# The
# Personal
# Efficiency
# Program

# The
# Personal
# Efficiency
# Program

## Fourth Edition

How to Stop Feeling Overwhelmed
and Win Back Control of Your Work!

Kerry Gleeson

**WILEY**
John Wiley & Sons, Inc.

*Tony D'Arcy—We are all better for having known you.*
*And in loving memory of our MorMor*

# CONTENTS

## CHAPTER 7

**Follow-Up and Follow-Through!    143**

## CHAPTER 11

### Making Meetings Effective    203

## CHAPTER 12

### Maintain It Now    217

# WORLDWIDE OPPORTUNITIES WITH IBT

The Personal Efficiency Program (PEP) was designed and developed in Sweden to help individuals and companies improve their workload management.

The Institute for Business Technology, incorporated in 1984 and whose corporate headquarters are located in the United States, was established to introduce the PEP throughout the world. Since its start, nearly 1,000,000 persons around the world have been trained and coached through the PEP process.

Licensed PEP consultants have delivered our coaching programs in more than 25 countries in Europe, the Asia Pacific Region, and North and South America. Opportunities for consultants abound in all of these regions.

As work pressure and stress exert their influence, an ever-growing number of organizations are using PEP as a tool to deal with the pressure and stress as well as to contribute to an increase in efficiency and productivity of their personnel.

There is virtually no limit to our PEP market. We work with a wide range of concerns from government ministries to multinational corporations to the local village baker.

IBT licenses PEP to qualified consultants who have been trained and supervised by us in the successful PEP coaching method. This method is not limited to entrepreneurs who want to market and deliver PEP but is also for organizations that want to bring PEP in house and have their own consultants implement PEP in their own organizations.

At the beginning of 2008, there were 350 active PEP coaches around the world.

If you are looking for a new career with great opportunities contact us at:

IBT International Inc.
PO Box 1057
Boca Raton, Florida 33429
USA
Tel: (1) 561 367 0467
Fax: (1) 561 367 0469
E-mail info@ibt-pep.com
Web site www.ibt-pep.com

# PREFACE

Overwhelmed is a word too often overheard in the office corridors and at the water cooler. With the proliferation of e-mail, technologies that enable us to be "on" 24 hours a day, cell phones, instant messenger, the Internet, text messaging, faxes (let's not forget paper), we are all feeling that we have too much to process and too little time to do it.

I have been in the white-collar productivity business for over a quarter of a century. I have seen increased pressure and demands placed on everyone trying to get their jobs done. You probably picked up this book because you recognized you need to do something!

In grappling with this problem, I have learned that the single biggest obstacle most people need to overcome has nothing to do with the amount of information you process or the demands placed on you, or even the amount of time you have. Your challenge will be in overcoming your own tendency to put things off that you don't like to do.

The vast majority of us have never been taught how to work.

Most of us have formed bad working habits, and those habits are hard to change.

Speaking of change—most of us do not like change very much.

Now in its fourth edition, this book has covered scores of technology changes over the years. But it is not the tech tips that will be important to you. What is important are the habits you have and the processes you use—how you form new and better habits and consistently improve on your personal work processes. This was true 25 years ago, and it is true now.

Changing habits and implementing effective personal work practices are what my company has been successfully doing for years. This book is the culmination of hundreds of experiences gleaned from the many highly effective people we at IBT have coached and trained over the past 25 years. What do these highly effective people do? How do they do it? Can their work behaviors be boiled down to principles everyone can apply? This book includes proven strategies developed to help our clients embrace these principles and make them part of their behaviors.

What makes up our personal work processes? How can you improve your organization? What systems work best? How can you get started quickly? How can you get organized quickly to get more done? All of this is covered in this book.

Furthermore, we have learned that e-mail and meetings are among the most wasteful activities for most of us. Fortunately, we have learned a good deal about how to deal with these two issues, and all of that experience and knowledge is now covered in two new chapters.

Many of us do not have the time to read. For those who want to "get on with it," I have added an "Executive Summary" chapter boiling down the basic process to a few pages.

Charles Dickens once said, "I never could have done what I have done without the habits of punctuality, order, and diligence." I hope you find the information in this book provides you with the knowledge and methodology to form new and better habits to create the best possible "order," encourage the use of tools to reinforce punctuality, and cultivate that magical quality, persistence, until you reach success.

KERRY GLEESON
*Boca Raton, Florida*

# ACKNOWLEDGMENTS

My thanks go to the many people who directly and indirectly made this book possible. This is the fourth edition; the book's initial publication was 15 years ago. Over the years, the number of people who have contributed to the book has grown. Its popularity today would not have been possible without the contributions of friends, clients, and business partners from the early years:

- To my agent/editors from Executive Excellence: Ken Shelton, Trent Price, and Meg McKay.
- To Richard Narramore, editor; Tiffany Groglio, editorial assistant; and my earlier John Wiley & Sons, Inc. editors Paula Sinnott, Linda Indig, Renana Myers, John Mahaney, and Mary Daniello.
- A special thanks goes to the many clients and friends who devoted time and effort to share their experiences. Clients Dagfinn Lunde, Eunice Johnson, John Birch, Hans Schmied, Frans Henrik Kockum, Kirk Stromber, Mike Gallico, and Mike Jercy went well out of their way to share their insights.
- My appreciation goes to all of the IBT staff and licensees who have enriched our client experiences and added many important points to this book.
- Many thanks to Bary and Lynn Sherman for their hard work and contributions to Chapter 9. Their years of helping customers succeed in mobile work environments have enriched this book and will, no doubt, help many people struggling to work in highly technical virtual offices.
- To Ira Chaleff, thank you! For all of the editing work and important advice that can be found throughout the book.

- To Lena (Holmberg) Davidsson, Jay Hurwitz, Eric Magnusson, Ron Hopkins, Peter Diurson, Menno van der Haven, Johan and Randi Holst, Bruno Savoyat, Denis Healy, Ann Searles, Mike and Lynn Valentine, Bouke Bouma, Sharon McGann, Benno Jangeborg, Margareta Norell, Catherine Bivar, Loes Nooij, Sonja Strich, Katharina Dietz, Susanne Lundberg, Jim Robinson, Michael Kongstad, Natascha Masius, Hans Wagenaar, Oleg Protsenko, Monica Ivesköld, Elisa Jensen Labiano, Margareta Hagstedt, Hans Wagenaar, and Monique Brinkman for their contributions, hard work, and dedication—thank you.
- A special thanks goes to Brita Norberg and Janita Thorner from Svenska Handlesbanken Sweden for the opportunity and help designing the original Personal Efficiency Program.
- And finally, to my wife Jill, and my children Brooke, Quinn, and Mackenzie, who have tolerated my behavior while writing this edition and provided the encouragement and support that made the book possible.

# INTRODUCTION

When people hear the word "efficiency," typically the first thought that comes to mind is "squeezing blood out of a stone." That is not my definition of efficiency. By efficiency, I mean how to get things done with the least amount of effort.

I have watched many new technologies enter the workplace and seen the positive effects of those devices. I have also seen how many of those new technologies have not lived up to people's expectations, and in many cases have made people more stressed and overwhelmed.

And it's not only the technologies that have profoundly affected people's work lives, but also the globalization of business. Nowadays, it's not uncommon to have people collaborating across continents and time zones, pushing work schedules from an 8-hour workday, to sometimes 16 or 18 hours on call. This new global business environment, along with the technologies, has added a new element of stress that didn't exist in the workforce even 10 years ago.

There used to be a time where you would receive a request through the post ("snail mail"), let it sit on your desk for a day or two, think about it, and even use the excuse that "It's in the mail." Now we have instant communications in the form of cell phones, instant messaging, and e-mail, and often we are expected to provide instant responses on almost anything. It seems everyone is demanding that more be done, and faster.

How does this affect people? It is not uncommon for me to find people in almost a constant state of being overwhelmed by their work. One person described it as an oppressive weight. People feel anxious, stressed, and out of control. These feelings certainly can't help get the work done.

I've found it's not the volume of work that affects people's feelings as much as how they do the work and respond to it that dramatically impacts how people feel about their work. I've seen people who have finally addressed this issue experience peace and relief. By looking at how they work, and improving on the work process, people end up in better control and experience greater success. The level of stress people experience is greatly diminished.

## ORIGIN OF THE PERSONAL EFFICIENCY PROGRAM

In the early 1980s, I was living in Sweden and had a small sales and marketing consulting business. To attract new clients, I devised a compensation plan unique to Sweden at the time. I wouldn't accept a fee unless the client achieved a specific measurable result. It had an attractive ring to it, and I found it easy to get companies interested and willing to at least see me and listen to what I had to say. If a potential client thought I had something to offer, the first hurdle to overcome was figuring out what constituted a measurable result. Since I specialized in sales and marketing, I could usually work out a measurable target, often in terms of increased sales and customers.

The next challenge I faced was creating a marketing and sales campaign that would deliver the measurable result. This was easier than I imagined: All I had to do was ask the people who did the work what they would do to reach the desired result. Most of the time they knew what they needed to do.

I would then develop a plan based on their input and give it to them. Interestingly, I would almost invariably return weeks later to find that the plan hadn't been executed. Staff members would say they didn't have time. They'd had too many other things to do; someone had been sick or went on holiday, or they'd simply forget. This posed a problem for me. I had to get them to execute the plan, or I wouldn't get paid. The workers would be caught up in day-to-day inefficiencies, wasting time looking for things, or disorganized in hundreds of ways, and I eventually saw that my main duty had little to do with sales and marketing. Instead, my primary role became getting the principals well organized so they could do the things they had been thinking about doing all along.

Before long, I succeeded in building up a client base. One of my clients was a branch of Svenska Handelsbanken, one of the most profitable banks in Scandinavia. The branch hired me to increase the amount of money in savings accounts—a measurable target. Along with the management team and staff, I worked out a marketing plan to accomplish their target. Then came the hard part—getting it done.

Several things were keeping the plan from being implemented. For example, as a matter of policy, bank personnel periodically rotated jobs and workstations. As a result, every few months, people would find themselves at a new workstation without knowing where things were. It would take a few weeks to attain some semblance of order. In the meantime, their time was wasted. Also, instead of processing each transaction immediately, some cashiers would create huge backlogs by setting aside the tasks they thought would take longer, and revisit them later. Cashiers who processed each task immediately didn't develop backlogs. Finally, since there were no baskets on the desks, when mail came in, it would be placed on the desk, often next to or on top of other papers already on the desk. Sometimes important items from the day's mail would get buried beneath other papers placed on the desk, or even overlooked entirely.

The branch manager was a competent executive, but she spent most of her time dealing with customers. This gave her little time to devote to organizing the work areas of individual workers.

I started a standard filing system at each desk and purged the place of clutter. That way, if someone had to use an unfamiliar workstation, at least he or she would know where to find things. I asked the senior cashier to describe how she processed her work. This became the model for processing branch transactions, and the other cashiers began to follow her model. We set up a central mail center with baskets for each worker. Soon, the staff was initiating their own solutions to common problems affecting their productivity. Eventually the bank hired me to package what I had done in this one branch and train 50 internal trainers to deliver the *Personal Efficiency Program* (PEP) to the bank's 500-branch network.

I learned from this experience, and from my many other clients in Sweden and a dozen other countries in Europe and North America, that although the vast majority of people are proficient and technically skilled to do their work, they don't understand the principles of work organization or the application of these principles to their jobs.

Most people think work process improvement is about improving the computer system or the manufacturing process. They may be only vaguely aware of their personal work process, and seldom, if ever, do they address how to improve that process.

The greatest success I had in improving group productivity came from focusing on the basics of the personal work process. Most people don't give much thought or assign much importance to the work process.

But, once they begin to work on *how* they do their work, they often continue without my encouragement because they become much more productive. William James, the famous nineteenth-century psychologist and philosopher, said, "What a person puts their mind to happens."

## HOW TO WORK

Most people have never been taught how to work. They go to college and get educated in their profession, go out into the workplace, and suddenly find themselves overwhelmed by paper and e-mail. How to process and deal with day-to-day activities and manage yourself at work is not something that schools teach.

So what do people do? They figure it out. How they manage their information and projects may or may not be the best way, but it's *their* way. Then, after many years of doing it their way over and over again, it becomes a habitual behavior. As time goes on, technologies change, and these now reinforced habits often become obstacles to adopting new ways of doing things or to taking advantage of new methods available to get things done more efficiently.

Many of us feel there isn't much we can do about market conditions, the organization, a difficult boss, or activities that are expected of us. It's human nature to view the cause of our difficulties as being outside of our control. The only hope for success is to focus our efforts on things we can do something about.

In my experience, one of the biggest obstacles to success is procrastination. Much of this book was written to help you overcome any tendencies you have to put things off.

Most people act when it's easy to do so. The better organized you are, the easier it is to act and the greater the tendency for you to do those things that should be done when they should be done, whether you like to or not. What you should act on is determined by how well you plan and how well you prioritize. This book identifies the processes you can apply to tighten up your planning and make it successful.

The advice you will find in this book is the culmination of the work of hundreds of coaches and years of experience on five continents, learning how people work, and coaching people on techniques that enable them to become more effective and more efficient in what they do.

The single most important lesson I hope you take from this book is the need to make continuous improvement in how you do what you do as part of your everyday work activities.

# CHAPTER 1
# Executive Summary

As a reader, you may simply want to understand the steps to take in order to apply the principles you will find throughout the rest of the book.

Our clients are always looking for ways to make their processes *leaner*. This is the equivalent of an executive overview to give you the highlights of how to make the Personal Efficiency Program (PEP) work for you in the minimal time needed to absorb its principles.

I summarize these steps in this "At a Glance" chapter for those who want to get on with it without having to study in detail the full content of the book.

To understand the reasoning and philosophy behind these steps, you can refer to the appropriate chapters in the book.

Meanwhile, if you follow these steps, I guarantee work will feel less overwhelming, you will soon gain more control over your day, get more done, and feel better about your work. You may need to customize the steps to fit the culture of your organization, or its technology, or your personal work style. That's fine. But be sure to follow the *principles* that are the basis of each recommended technique.

The PEP process begins with self-management. The questions you must keep in the forefront of your mind are: "How do I do what I do?" and "How can I do it better?"

The most common work mistake people make is putting things off that they don't like to do—procrastination. Most of us do not procrastinate consciously. Mostly, procrastination is a bad habit. An enormous amount of time is consumed simply going over (mentally or otherwise) all the things to be done, instead of acting in the first place.

People tend to act when it's easy to do so. The aim of the PEP process is to make it easier for you to act—in other words, to get you organized so you can act sooner.

## GET ORGANIZED

To get organized, begin by purging your existing organizational structure. Clear the clutter—physical and mental.

Set aside a block of uninterrupted time. A few hours should be enough to get started.

Begin by emptying the drawer that will become your "working file" or "active drawer" so you can create organized files there. (On subsequent days, you can schedule in your calendar to continue the process on your reference file drawers).

Empty everything from your drawers, file cabinets, paper trays, walls, briefcase, and so on—every piece of paper—and place it all on your desk. Look everywhere: under the blotter, behind the curtain, under the desk. Gather all your papers and pile them indiscriminately on top of your desk. Begin going through each and every one of the papers to sort them. Deal with them as follows:

- Pick up the top piece of paper and deal with it now in one of the following ways:
    - If it is something that needs to done and will only take a few minutes, deal with it to completion—now.
    - If it is something to be done that might take you some time to complete, write or type it into your task list as something to be done. If you use Personal Information Manager (PIM) software, such as Microsoft Outlook or Lotus Notes, use the "To Do" function to write the task down. Your aim is to write down all the things that need to be done in one place. (When you write it down, identify what is the specific next step to be done on the task so that it is clear what you need to do next when you finally get to it.)
    - Once you have either done or identified what needs to be done with that piece of paper, sort it. If the paper reflects future work, start setting up a pile on the floor called "Working Files." If the paper represents something that you may need to access again in the future, create a second pile called "Reference Materials."
    - If the paper represents something that should be delegated, forward it to the correct person. (If it is something that you want to follow up on, make a note in your task list to do so.)
    - If the paper can be found elsewhere, either electronically or otherwise, and it isn't something that you know you will need to use in the future, throw it away or shred it.

Carry on with this process, paper by paper, until the desktop is empty and two piles exist on the floor for all the Working Files and Reference Materials you intend to keep.

Next organize your Working File pile. Sort through and identify the key categories that represent the papers in your pile. It might be "Project X" or it might be a category called "Finance" and within it, a subcategory called "Budget." Use a piece of paper to write down the names of the general categories. Chapter 3 provides a process we call

"Responsibility Mapping" to identify key categories that represent your main job functions. You shouldn't have more than 8 or 10 high-level categories or you will not be able to create a pattern you can easily remember. They will become alphabetical instead of subject oriented. Once you have identified the categories, create hanging folders and tabs for each, and place the "Working Files" into the drawer of the desk closest to where you sit.

Apply the same process to the pile of Reference Materials.

Now that your papers are organized, move to the computer. Your e-mail program will likely have the capability of creating folders enabling you to organize and find again those e-mails that you wish to keep. If you don't already know how to do so, familiarize yourself with how to create folders for saved e-mail. Sort your inbox e-mail by date, and beginning with the oldest e-mail, process each as follows:

- If the e-mail can be responded to and completed within a few minutes, do it now.
- If the e-mail can be delegated, delegate it now.
- If the e-mail requires some time to process, add it to your task list, noting the specific next step required. Outlook, Lotus Notes, and other PIMs often allow you to move the e-mail into a task, in which case, do so, and fill in the parameters including the specific next step on the subject line, and a reminder if you want to be prompted to act at a certain time to do it. (Categorize the task so that you are able to sort and view new tasks by subject matter.)
- If the e-mail is something you need to keep for future reference, create a folder under the inbox (the folder name should be consistent with the folders you've created in your Working Files). Drag the e-mail into the appropriate folder. (These folders should only be created under the inbox if your organization has no limit on the size of files you can keep in your inbox. In many organizations there is a limit so the folder structure needs to be created in another space. You should consult with your IT department as needed to identify what that space should be. If it is a drive that is not backed up automatically, you will also need to consult with IT to establish a backup process.)
- If the e-mail is not something you need to keep for future reference, delete it.
- Follow these steps until your inbox is empty, your task list represents everything you need to do that came to you in the form

of e-mail, and your folder tree is created with those e-mails you intend to save for future reference.

- *Note:* If you have more than a couple hundred messages, you should pick a date (maybe two to four months back) and move everything older into a folder you create called "Old Mail" and just leave it there for a couple of months. You can delete the whole folder once you are convinced you are no longer going into it to find anything. Then apply the PEP e-mail process just described to the mail still in the inbox. This will make it easier and quicker for you to process what is still current.

Organize the documents on your hard drive. If you are a Microsoft user, go into "Documents" and create categories that mirror your paper files and e-mail folder tree. For documents you intend to keep, drag and drop into the appropriate folder.

At this point, your desk should be clear of its paper. The paper should be organized in a way that makes it easy to find what you need to find. Your electronic documents should be better organized than they were before. Your e-mail inbox should be empty. All of the things that you need to do should be tasked.

Your newly organized state should make it easy to act.

## HABITS AND ROUTINES

> *The secret of success of every man who has ever been successful—lies in the fact that he formed the habit of doing things that failures don't like to do.*
> —ALBERT E. N. GRAY, "The Common Denominator of Success"

The single most important rule to follow when it comes to processing your work is to act on a task or item the first time you touch or see it. The mantra of PEP is *Do It Now.* Of course, not everything can be done now, and possibly not everything should be done now. Your aim, however, should be acting on the item the first time you run across it. If you are not going to do something, don't look at it. If you look at it, do it now.

A technique that can be employed to reinforce this "look and act once" concept is called *batching.* Many elements of your work can be reduced to simple routines that will let you complete similar tasks in the shortest possible time.

A case in point is e-mail. E-mail is not for instant communication. A visit to the office or a telephone call or, depending on the culture, an instant message, should be employed if something needs to be done instantly. Batch e-mail, that is, schedule two or three times a day to process your e-mail completely. Do not look at e-mail any other time. Turn off your e-mail alerts, and instead schedule a time (possibly first thing in the morning, then again after lunch, and finally before you go home) to view and process your e-mail completely. If your organization culture seems to demand more immediate turnaround of e-mail, this should be raised in departmental meetings because it means that everyone needs to interrupt everything they are doing continuously when e-mail arrives even if it is of relatively low importance.

When processing e-mail, follow the four Ds:

1. *Do it now.* Read, respond, and act on the e-mail to completion.
2. *Delegate it.* If it's something that someone else can or should do, pass it on to them now.
3. *Designate it.* Create a task if it's something that's going to take you some time to do. Use a calendar to schedule the task.
4. *Discard (or file) it.*

By following the four Ds you will have processed each e-mail and at the end have an empty inbox.

One more note: Most e-mail applications allow for the screening of incoming e-mail. In Outlook and Lotus Notes, you can establish "Rules" to eliminate less important messages or batch routine messages into folders that can be looked at once or twice a week, and so on. If you are getting a couple hundred e-mail messages a day this is essential.

## BATCHING WORK

Analyze all of your work. Identify the things you do that can be batched such as telephone calls, e-mail, follow-up activities, paying bills, reading, routine paperwork, filing, meetings with direct reports, and any other routine functions.

Once you have established the types of work that can be batched, set up simple routines in your schedule to act on these batched activities.

You are now organized so that it's easier to act, find things, and get things done. You have a complete list of all your to-do activities.

You have established routines to process work in a more organized (batched) way. The next step is task management or planning.

## PLANNING

People tend to act when they have a clear picture (idea) of what it is that they need to do. The purpose of planning is to provide you with clear pictures.

The components of *planning* include:

- Having clearly stated goals and objectives;
- Breaking down into specific tasks the steps that will lead you to the accomplishment of your goals and objectives;
- Managing tasks—consistent review, prioritization, follow-up, and follow through; and
- Rebuilding the plans that failed to meet the goals and objectives and persisting until you achieve them.

My advice is to establish a routine time in your calendar once a week to go through all of your outstanding tasks and identify which ones need to be done and or progressed in the next week. Compare these tasks to your calendar activities for the next week, other scheduled activities (meetings, etc.), deadlines that must be met (or milestones to those deadlines) and estimate how much time you can devote to your tasks in the upcoming week. Prioritize the items that need to be done and identify your list of tasks for the upcoming week. We call this *Weekly Review and Action Plan* (WRAP).

If you find yourself hesitating on a task or project, you probably don't have a clear idea of what it is that needs to be done. Break the task down into its smallest possible components. Pick up the first thing that you need to do and note that down in your weekly task list.

If you have staff who report to you, keep in mind tasks you have delegated don't necessarily get done simply because you ask to have them done. Typically you need to follow through on things that you've delegated, items that you're waiting for, and so on. Part of your task list for the new week should include a follow-up of those tasks you have delegated to make sure they get done.

Finally, expand the use of your calendar. If you want to get something done, schedule it. This is an old and proven time management rule. Too often, people's use of a calendar is limited to scheduling meetings/appointments. Your calendar should also include reminders, deadlines, and milestones. Schedule time in your calendar to do your most important tasks.

## CONTINUOUS IMPROVEMENT OF THE PROCESS (*KAIZEN*)

Continuous improvement is the philosophical basis for PEP. The time-tested steps in this chapter can improve how you do what you do. It is possible your exact situation may not be reflected in these steps. That does not matter. The real outcome of PEP is not necessarily a neat person, or even a better-organized or more efficient person. Nor do you have to follow these steps to be successful in your work. The important outcome of PEP is making continuous improvement of your personal work processes part of your everyday activities.

So, if you find a part of your work at all difficult or problematic, ask yourself how you can do it more easily the next time and act immediately on the answer to that question.

Most of us manage to do our work one way or another. Whether we are managing it in the most efficient or effective way possible is the question we should ask ourselves. In many years of working with highly effective and efficient people, I have found one common factor among those who manage to get things done—they're always looking for the waste in their activities and testing ways to eliminate it.

The steps described in this chapter are simple, yet at the same time many people are challenged to do them without a coach to guide and even push them through this. PEP training has been popular because it provides facilitation. You can simulate this by teaming up with one or more staff, setting aside a day or half day to begin this process, and helping each other stay focused on getting through the steps. You can even have contests for "Most Organized," "Most Improved," and "Most Innovative." Then be sure to schedule a follow-up day because you almost certainly will have more to do in order to extend the process to older files or deeper levels of planning. Remember *Kaizen* and *do it now!*

# CHAPTER 2
# Do It Now!

*Lose this day loitering—'twill be the same story*
*Tomorrow—and the next more dilatory;*
*Each indecision brings its own delays,*
*And days are lost lamenting o'er lost days.*
*Are you earnest? seize this very minute—*
*Boldness has genius, power and magic in it.*

*Only engage, and then the mind grows heated—*
*Begin it, and the work will be completed!*
*—JOHANN WOLFGANG VON GOETHE*

# Chapter 2 Preview

In this chapter, you will learn how to:

- Get more done by doing it now.
- Overcome procrastination by getting in the habit of acting.
- Reduce your workload by doing the work once.
- Become more decisive by looking at the worst possible consequence of your action and then getting on with it if you could live with that consequence.
- Stop using priorities as an excuse not to do things.
- Start thinking: It is either important enough to do or it isn't; if it's important, then I'll act on it; if it's not important, I won't do it.
- Be as clever about completing things as you are about putting things off.

*I hear and I forget. I see and I remember. I do and I understand.*
—CONFUCIUS

Now! No doubt you hear the word all the time. If not from your boss, your spouse, or your child, you hear it from advertisers and salespeople. Some days it seems everyone and everything is demanding something *now*. A manager or coworker tells you someone didn't show up for work and what she was doing needs to be done by you, now. Or someone from home calls to tell you a pipe is leaking, now. Or the telephone rings and demands to be picked up, now. An advertisement tells you to buy it, now. People and things demand our time and attention now, this moment, immediately. And so we find ourselves buried in our work, in spite of all the nice time management theories and tools.

Some time management gurus tell us we should ignore all the things that clamor for our urgent attention, including the telephone. They tell us we shouldn't react to circumstances and people around us; instead, we should organize, prioritize, and gain control of our lives by putting off some tasks and focusing our attention on those activities that are "most important," or "first things," or "top priorities."

Planning, setting goals, and priorities have a place. But too often when we set priorities, we don't get around to everything on our lists. "Less important" activities get shoved into the closet by "more urgent" activities. Eventually the "less important" things rot there. Not surprisingly, when they start to stink, they become very high priorities. And guess who has to clean up the mess? You do, of course, *now!*

## WHY THE PERSONAL EFFICIENCY PROGRAM WORKS

The only method I've found that really produces the results people want (the method you're going to learn here) is to gain the advantage by getting the "now" on your side. I call it the *Do It Now* approach to personal efficiency.

By *choosing* to *Do It Now,* you make *now* your ally, not your enemy. So, what do you do about the mess that accumulates on your desk? You *Do It Now.* Doing it now enables you to be better organized; to exercise greater control over the when, where, and how of what you're doing; and to feel better about yourself and your performance. Not surprisingly, *Do It Now* is the first tenet of the Personal Efficiency Program (PEP).

*The beginning is the half of every action.*
— GREEK PROVERB

Does the following scenario sound familiar?

You arrive at the office, sit down, turn on your computer, and open your e-mail. You have 250 messages in the inbox—many of them have been there for days or weeks. The subject line of one from Mary reminds you, "Oh, I need to call Mary." Dutifully, you make a mental note to remember and move to the next e-mail. This one is a complaint from a customer. You think, "I should answer this today." You go to the next e-mail, and you see that it represents a problem, and you think, "I've got to talk to my boss about this." You look at the next e-mail and say, "This isn't important; I can do it later." And so it goes, on and on. You end up shuffling through scores of e-mail and stacks of paper representing your things to do, and, by the time you get back to the top of your e-mail and reread each item you intended to do, you have wasted time reading everything twice, doubling the time it takes but accomplishing little.

This procedure would almost be okay if we only went through it twice. But too many of us look at our e-mail and mail three, four, or five times before we ever act on them. It takes a lot longer to do something five times than it does to do it once.

The first rule for improving personal efficiency is:

*Act on an item the first time you read or touch it.*

I'm not talking about those things that you can't do now or even those things you shouldn't do now. I'm talking about all the things that you could and should do, but you don't. I'm talking about routine paperwork and e-mail of the sort you encounter every day. Take care of these things the first time you touch or read them, and you'll save yourself a lot of time in the long run.

Call Mary. Respond to that e-mail message immediately. Answer the customer's letter of complaint. Act on that voice mail as you listen. Talk to the boss about the problem. *Do It Now.* You'll be amazed at how little time it actually takes and how good you feel when it's done.

If you're not going to act on your paperwork, don't waste time looking at it. If you're not going to return your voice mail messages, don't waste time listening to them. If you're not going to respond to your e-mail messages, don't waste time looking at them. Don't clog up your day with things you *aren't* going to do. Instead, move on to what you *are* going to do, and *Do It Now*.


## START WITH YOUR DESK OR WORK SPACE

***Postpone not a good action.***

**—IRISH PROVERB**


When people ask for my help in getting organized and putting PEP in place in their work and their lives, the first thing I do is put them through a personal desk cleaning. I actually go to the person's desk and go through all the bits and pieces of paper with them. I begin with paper even though electronic communication and documents are quickly taking over as the medium of choice in business. The reason is people can more easily conceptualize with paper than with documents they cannot touch. I'll pick up a paper and ask what it is. They say, "Uh, well, that's something I was supposed to respond to."

"Okay," I say. Then they naturally start to put it somewhere, but I stop them. "Hold it a second. Why are you putting it over there?"

They give me an incredulous look and say, "Well, I have to do it, so I put it over there."

"Well, let's *Do It Now*."

"You want me to *Do It Now*? It could take some time."

"I don't mind. I'll sit here while you do it."

And they do it. Usually I clock it. And I say, "How long did that take?"

"One minute," they say, or "three minutes," or whatever.

"Look at that," I tell them. "See?"

"Yeah," they say. "It didn't take much time at all."

And I say, "I was hoping you'd notice that."

When this task is done the first time, it makes people uncomfortable. They do it, but they usually haven't grasped the concept yet, even though we talk about it and ask them to commit themselves to the concept and the work style. What they don't understand is that *Do It Now* is meant to be permanent and ongoing.

Even if they remember *Do It Now* and believe they follow the principle in the beginning, they are often inconsistent in their application of the *Do It Now* concept.

This is evident when I go back for a follow-up visit. Usually, they've cleaned up their office or work space in anticipation of my coming, with everything stacked neatly into piles. They're very proud they've mastered the concept. After all, it's easy enough to talk about *Do It Now* and even to get a person to agree with it. But most people think they *Do It Now* when they don't. Only by working with this concept consistently over time—as I do—do you begin to see more and more evidence of *not* acting the first time and all the reasons people make up for why they can't or shouldn't act now.

A first visit with one client included a thorough desk cleaning. We worked through every item on his desk, one at a time, until everything had been done that could be done. We talked about acting on things the first time—about doing it now—and he was so impressed that he committed himself to *Do It Now* as his new work philosophy.

When I went back for a follow-up visit, I hardly made it through the door before he started telling me that *Do It Now* was the greatest thing that had ever happened to him—it was just marvelous. He was very enthusiastic about the program and about the change it had made in his life.

Then I picked up the papers from his pending basket. The first was a phone message. I said, "Why don't we call him now?"

He frowned just a little. "Now?" he said.

And I said, "Yes."

And so he picked up the phone and returned the call. By the end of our meeting, we'd gone through every single piece of paper in his pending basket.

Why was I able to empty his pending basket when he hadn't been able to? Because his definition of *pending* was something to be done later, and one visit with PEP obviously hadn't changed that.

Let me emphasize what I mean: *Do It Now* means *Do It Now,* regularly and consistently, day after day. Not doing it now is what got you into trouble in the first place. Your pending basket is strictly for things you *can't* do now, for things that are out of your control. For example, you call Mary back on Monday because that's when she's back from vacation, not because Monday seems like a good day to do it. *That's* pending.

Grasp the concept of *Do It Now* and the real meaning of pending— and function accordingly each and every day—and these simple words will literally change the way you approach your work and your life. You'll find yourself getting more work done than ever before.

# OVERCOMING PROCRASTINATION

*Procrastination is the thief of time.*
—EDWARD YOUNG

Simple procrastination probably eats up more time in the workplace than anything else. If you're a procrastinator, you'll find *Do It Now* is a key element in helping you to identify where procrastination exists in your work habits and helping you to overcome it.

Most people are very clever, even ingenious, about putting things off. "I don't have time" is a common excuse. "I think they said they're not going to be there today, so I didn't bother to call." "This could take forever, so I had better wait until I have a free day to start." "It's not so important." The list of reasons why a task can't be completed is endless.

My approach is this: *Be as clever about completing things as you've been about putting them off.* So Mary's not there. Who else could give you the information? Her assistant? Where else could you get this information? Who could this task be delegated to? How can you get this job done? That is the point, isn't it—how you can get that letter, that folder, or that report out of your in basket and off of your desk so that you never have to look at it again? That's where you should focus your brainpower—not on clever excuses.

*How soon not now, becomes never.*
—MARTIN LUTHER

This may sound simple, but it's a bitter pill to swallow: Too often the reason you're not getting things done is that you're just not doing them. You can reverse that trend, though, starting now—right now—by learning how to overcome procrastination and to increase your personal productivity. How? The following eight ways to overcome procrastination can benefit you immediately and immensely.

1. *Do It Once.* Sorting through all the papers on your desk and creating To Do and Do Later piles for yourself is a common practice. You have plenty of company if you're a pile creator. One woman I know goes through this creating piles process regularly. The first time through she calls it "reading for familiarity." The second read-through is her "action" read, unless she sets it aside "to do later." Now, this woman is a two-time cum laude graduate of a prestigious university, handling

a responsible position in business! By adopting and implementing *Do It Now* she could immediately experience the most immediate benefit of PEP: *Do It Now,* and you do it once.

Needlessly rereading everything on your desk or in your e-mail before acting on it achieves nothing. You know what's required the first time you read a customer's letter of complaint. Reading the letter twice only doubles your reading time and the letter is still not answered. Answer the letter the first time you read through it—*Do It Now*—and you save time, move toward customer satisfaction, and accomplish a task that otherwise prevents you from doing more important things.

2. *Clear Your Mind.* A client once described to me what it was like for him to drive home from work at the end of the day. When he would drive past a gas station, he would think: "I must get a spare tire for my car. I had a flat some time ago and have not gotten around to getting the spare." On he would drive past a pharmacy and think: "Vitamin C. We need Vitamin C. Winter is coming, and we need it for the expected sniffles." He would drive past a supermarket and think: "My wife wanted me to pick up bread. Ah, I don't feel like it." By the time he got home, he was exhausted. He told me he would be breathing hard. He needed a drink to calm down. "Everything I looked at reminded me of things I hadn't done!" he said. Mind you, not once did he stop and do any of those things. But he sure felt as if he had worked hard on these things. He was exhausted from procrastination.

Consider how many tasks and projects you have connected with your work. One hundred? Two hundred? Now consider how many tasks, incomplete activities, and wish-list items you have connected with your family. How many tasks or wish-list items could you list that are connected with your hobbies, your friends, as well as civic, church, or other groups you belong to? As you add these up, you'll discover that the outstanding items—the things taking up space in your mind—probably number five hundred to one thousand.

> *Think only what is right there, what is right under your nose to do. It's such a simple thing—that's why people can't do it.*
> —**HENRY MILLER**

Experience tells us that we're limited in how many tasks or activities our minds can juggle at any given time. How does this affect your work? Let's use the example of a customer's letter or e-mail. You look at the first line: "Can you please send me some information about a new product?" Immediately your attention flies off to the information you were supposed to send to someone else but haven't gotten around to yet. You drag your attention back and read a bit further. "Can you meet with some of my colleagues to discuss a certain project?" Again your attention wanders off to several other meetings you need to prepare for but haven't gotten to yet. Once again you drag your attention back to the task at hand. The sheer volume of incomplete activities in your life distracts you from concentrating on and completing what's in front of you. This is where priorities fit into the picture.

Obviously, prioritizing can be an important part of controlling your work. But prioritizing can also be the best excuse *not* to do something. Prioritizing means that "unimportant" tasks get pushed off until later and may not ever get done at all. The consequence of not doing tasks in a timely way is your inability to focus on the work at hand because of the voices in your head reminding you of uncompleted tasks.

Have you ever kept a list of 10 things to do, only to have the bottom five never change? We tend to focus on top-priority items and neglect lower-priority items. That's why we call them lower priority, yet we still consider these things to be important.

My view is that things either should or should not be done. If deadlines are involved, certainly they must be considered, but if something is important enough to do, do it. Otherwise, don't.

The best way to eliminate task overload is to eliminate these little things that make you feel overloaded and that pull your attention away from your major tasks. Act on these smaller, "less important" tasks. Make a list of all of them, set aside some quiet time, and do them one by one. Or decide not to do one and trash it. Better yet, get yourself organized using the ideas in this book and don't allow tasks to accumulate in the first place.

With this overload eliminated, you're no longer distracted. Your level of concentration increases and, accordingly, you not only finish more tasks, you finish them better and more quickly than before. Komar was reported to have said:

*Concentration, in its truest, unadulterated form, means being able to focus the mind on one single solitary thing.*

If you can concentrate—focus—on what you are trying to do, you will bring to bear on the task one of the most critical elements of success.

3. *Solve Problems While They're Small.* As you gain experience in a job, you learn to detect those little red flags that tell you something is wrong and will only get worse unless you take action. The question becomes: When and how do I act on these small indicators? Unfortunately, we tend to ignore these red flags too often in the face of more pressing issues.

Sometimes I point out a questionable stack of papers on the corner of someone's desk. Rather sheepishly, the person admits, "It's my problem pile. I figure if they sit there long enough, they'll go away." And sometimes they do.

You've heard of Murphy's Law. In England it's called Sod's Law: If anything can go wrong, it will. There's a corollary to Murphy's Law: If 10 things can go wrong with something, you can be sure the thing that will cause the most damage will be the one that goes wrong! Maybe most of those items in your problem pile will go away if you let them sit long enough. But you can be sure the one problem you don't want to happen will be the one that happens. And how much longer will it take you to take care of a crisis than to take care of the warning flag?

Get into the habit of acting on these things now, and you'll catch problems when they're still small, before they become big, time-consuming crises. As a result, you'll have more time to concentrate on the important things.

4. *Reduce Interruptions.* Most people admit they have a hard time avoiding or preventing interruptions. Instead, interruptions are seen as something beyond the control of mortals and the cause of nearly all our problems. How often have you heard or said, "Well, I would have gotten it done if I hadn't been interrupted every time I turned around!"

I remember a time I did some work for a bank in Luxembourg. I delivered my coaching services and sent an invoice. Two months later I hadn't received payment. I called the managing director, and his response was, "I did it now!"—with a chuckle—"I signed the invoice and sent it to the accounts payable department." We both got a laugh out of that and I said I would talk to the accounts payable department. I followed up with a young lady in that department. By telephone, in my typical American way, I asked, "Where's my money?" She said, "I am so sorry you haven't been paid. But I have been so busy explaining to people why they haven't been paid that I haven't had the time to pay the bills."

All too often, the interruptions people complain about are the result of their not having done something in the first place. Consequently, they not only have the work itself to do, but they also have to deal with those people who depended on that work being done, which only creates more work. Furthermore, most of us don't relish having to explain why we haven't done something. Even if you have a perfectly good reason, and the person on the other end of the phone sympathizes with you, you'll be left with a bad taste in your mouth just because you had to beg off one more time with an excuse and an explanation.

If you want to avoid interruptions, do the tasks related to them. You can then spend more time on your work and less time explaining why you haven't done it. Gain a reputation for completing work on time, and you'll reduce interruptions further by eliminating those bothersome requests for interim project status reports.

Mind you, some interruptions are desirable. If a sale depends on immediate feedback, of course the sales manager wants to be interrupted. Eliminating unnecessary interruptions and not aggravating the situation by creating reasons for others to interrupt you is what I'm referring to. Other benefits to eliminating these self-created interruptions are the improved quality of your work when you're free to concentrate on it fully and your ability to complete more work in the same amount of time because you're able to work undisturbed.

5. *Clean Up Backlogs.* If you have to keep up with an ongoing heavy work flow and, at the same time, you have an accumulation of backlogs, you must address the backlogs if you're to get your work flow under control. Remember, backlogs create their own additional work, so eliminating them cuts down your workload more than you may imagine at first. Here are five essential steps for handling backlogs:

1. Identify the backlogs.
2. Prioritize what backlogs to clean up first.
3. Schedule time each day to take a piece of a backlog and clean it up.
4. Identify the cause of the backlog.
5. Take steps to remedy the cause to prevent the backlog from happening again and to prevent any further buildup of backlogs.

Once we clean up old backlogs and prevent logjams from happening, we'll be better able to look to the future.

6. *Start Operating toward the Future instead of in the Past.* Figure 2.1 illustrates what occurs mentally when you have lots of past due, incomplete, or old tasks yet to be done. The Xs on the diagram

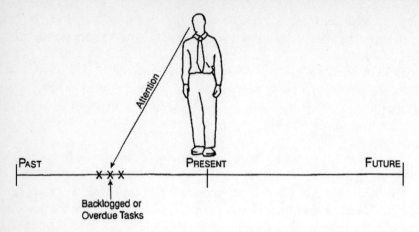

**Figure 2.1** Attention focuses on the past, not the future, with a backlog of tasks.

symbolize all of the tasks that should have been done some time in the past. Your focus is clouded by being dragged back into the past. Psychologists say that one indication of a person's mental health is the degree to which they operate in the past as opposed to operating in the present and future. Operating from the present toward the future is considered healthy. No wonder we can feel a bit crazy when we are overwhelmed with so many overdue tasks.

> *Nothing is so fatiguing as the eternal hanging-on of an uncompleted task.*
>
> **—William James**

When you are operating in the past, you tend to focus on what might have been, on lost opportunities. Anything that directs you from the present toward the future is healthier than that which drags you back in time.

Suppose you are running a race in which the starting line is Present and the finish line is Future. If rather than starting the race at Present you start from the Past, you have that much farther to run just to get to the starting line.

Figure 2.2 illustrates how cleaning up those tasks that attract our attention to the past frees up attention capacity for the present. This is important because we all have limited attention capacity—much less

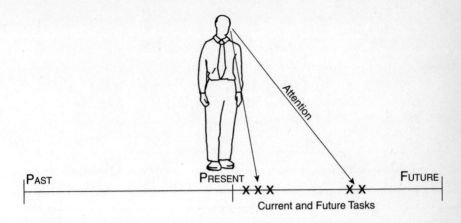

PAST                    PRESENT                    FUTURE

**X X X**            **X X**

Current and Future Tasks

**Figure 2.2** When backlogs are cleaned up, it is much easier to concentrate on current and future tasks.

capacity than we might imagine. Attention is critical to getting to the meat of the matter and pushing things through to completion.

> *Life is denied by lack of attention, whether it be to cleaning windows or trying to write a masterpiece.*
> —NADIA BOULANGER

7. *Stop Worrying about It.* It's one thing to waste time doing things over again or dealing with added interruptions or bigger fires, but the real harm of putting things off is how it affects you mentally and emotionally.

Almost everyone tends to put off unpleasant tasks. Facing up to your unpleasant tasks and completing them isn't easy, but the consequences of *not* doing them can be much worse than simply dealing with the unpleasantness early.

> *The greatest amount of wasted time is the time not getting started.*
> —DAWSON TROTMAN

To compound the problem, most people who procrastinate not only don't do the task, they also tend to dwell on the unfinished or undone task and worry about not having done it. This worry consumes far more time than people may realize. And it makes it harder to take causative action to solve the problem.

Think of some of the problems you've faced in the past. Did dwelling on them get you anywhere? No. It was only when you finally initiated some action that the problem began to be resolved. If you face up to the big problems and unpleasant tasks and do something about them, they usually vanish rather quickly.

> *The dread of doing a task uses up more time and energy than doing the task itself.*
> —RITA EMMETT

I once worked with a group of highly educated, bright, young service technicians from a large company in Denmark. I noticed a large machine on the corner of one of their desks and asked about it. The technician replied, "That's a bit of bad conscience. I received it from a customer a month ago to repair and I haven't repaired it yet."

I said, "That's terrible!"

He said, "I know. I've thought about it a lot, but I'm so busy that I haven't had the time to repair it. It could take me two days to fix it, and my schedule is so tight I haven't been able to devote the time to it." He went on to say, "As a matter of fact, you could help me."

"How?" I asked.

He said, "You could tell my boss how busy I am."

Well, my help took a little different direction. I said, *"Do It Now."*

"I can't *Do It Now,"* he argued. "I have a meeting at two o'clock, and..."

"Okay. Just *Do It Now,* and let's see how far you get," I suggested.

Well, off he went into the repair area with the machine, muttering to himself. Fifteen minutes later he came back.

"Oh, no," I thought. "This could be trouble."

He looked at me and said, "It's done."

"Done?" I echoed.

"Yes, done," he said. "But it could have taken two days."

Of course, we don't always get so lucky. It could have taken two days to repair. But how often have similar things happened to all of us? When you finally get down to the business of doing something you've been putting off, it isn't nearly as bad as you thought it might be.

*The shortest answer is doing.*
——GEORGE HERBERT

Most of us tend to exaggerate how long an unpleasant task will take or how unpleasant it really is. We dread doing it, so we put it off. Here was a man who had put off a job for a month, with the machine sitting there on his desk as a reminder of the thing he dreaded. He'd let it become a sore spot in his conscience and a sore spot between him and his boss. And rather than giving the task the 15 minutes it actually required, he'd been blaming his boss for his being too busy. In fact, he'd been procrastinating, but regardless of the cause, the customer hadn't received service and had been without the machine for a month.

The trick? Face up to the unpleasant tasks and *act* on them *now*.

M. Scott Peck, in his book *The Road Less Traveled* (Simon & Schuster, 1978), calls acting on unpleasant tasks "delaying gratification." Peck points out that life is difficult. People who procrastinate tend to want immediate gratification. Peck says:

*Delaying gratification is a process of scheduling the pain and pleasure of life in such a way as to enhance the pleasure by meeting and experiencing the pain first and getting it over with. It is the only decent way to live.*

What tasks in your own work would you treat on a "worst first" basis? Committing to a *Do It Now* mentality will help you overcome your resistance to dealing with unpleasant tasks. It will help you tackle the things you don't relish doing with a determination to have them over and done with. Some people take an almost perverse pride in being able to deal with the ugliest, meanest, most difficult things first. Most of us can improve our ability to handle the difficult head-on. Remember what Mark Twain said: "If you have to swallow two frogs, swallow the big one first, and don't look at it too long." So, if you can choose the sequence of your work each day, choose the task you enjoy least and do it first. Not only will the second task of the day be not quite so bad compared to the first, but completing the worst first tends to give your self-confidence a boost.

8. *Now, Feel Better about Yourself.* Dr. Linda Sapadin in her book *It's about Time* (Penguin Books, 1997) says:

*Procrastination inevitably diminishes one's self-esteem, which results in a loss of optimism, happiness, and creative energy. People who suffer from chronic procrastination and do nothing about it find it increasingly difficult to strive toward personal goals or, often, even to formulate them.*

Procrastination and attendant cover-ups create a buildup of negative emotions not always evident on the surface. In one PEP course, a newly married young woman began to laugh almost uncontrollably when the subject of procrastination was brought up. When asked what prompted this reaction she said:

*Oh, I was thinking about my husband's ruffled shirt. You see, I hate ironing, particularly my husband's shirt with the ruffled front. I would pull all the other items in the ironing basket out from under this shirt and do them first.*

When asked, "What happens when this shirt is the only thing left?" her response was, "Oh, I throw it back in the washing machine! My husband can't ever figure out where his favorite shirt has gone." A tremendous amount of emotional buildup comes with this habit of procrastination. It has strong impact on one's self-image.

By committing to *Do It Now,* completing the hard jobs first, and handling the big jobs bite-by-bite, you'll trim a tremendous load of stress and anxiety from your work. You'll gain more self-confidence and self-respect. Even after completing only one day of PEP participants have processed and purged all of the papers and documents on and in their desks, their file drawers, and their computers. They discover that they can accomplish much more than they ever realized before. They no longer have a guilty conscience. Almost instantly participants feel better about themselves.

## NOT EVERYTHING CAN OR SHOULD BE DONE NOW

> *Knowing when not to work hard is as important as knowing when to.*
>
> —HARVEY MACKAY, *Swim with the Sharks without Being Eaten Alive* (Ballantine Books, 1988)

Having said a lot about doing things now, let me point out that it isn't always possible or desirable to do everything now. You try to call Mary, but she won't be in until Monday. You're on your way to get coffee when a client calls about business. Clearly priorities do play an important part in productive work and in achieving results. However, ultimately success comes from getting things done. And too often people don't get things done because they don't do them! They do not *act now*.

In fact, priorities can be the best excuse a person has not to do something. Yes, there will be times you can't *Do It Now*. There will be times you shouldn't *Do It Now*. Common sense is a necessity; it should be a given. The way to increase your personal efficiency is not to *Do Something Stupid Now*. However, if your approach toward work is to always choose, always prioritize, always give it some time to ripen, always have an excuse to look at it later, always shuffle through your papers or scan through your e-mail, you are *not* acting. In fact, you are reinforcing the habit of not acting. With *Do It Now* and no more excuses to procrastinate, the end product is a propensity to *act*.

## BUILD DECISIVENESS INTO YOUR WORK HABITS

*In a moment of decision, the best thing you can do is the right thing to do. The worst thing you can do is nothing.*
— **THEODORE ROOSEVELT**

Successful people in general take little time to make a decision but take a long time to change a decision once it has been made.

Many people are afraid to be decisive. After all, if you make a decision, you have to live with the consequences. If decisiveness is a weak spot with you, there's an easy way to help you handle the quandary. Simply imagine the worst possible consequences of any decision you can make, and ask yourself if you can live with those consequences. If the answer is "yes," go for it.

You can't expect to be 100% certain of your course of action at all times. I understand, though, that George Patton, the famous World War II American general, worked with the following formula for success: "If you have a plan you're 80% certain of, you should violently execute it."

9. *Develop Decisiveness in Decision Making*. Realize that, beyond a certain point, the time you take to make a decision does not improve the chances that the decision will be correct. Accept the fact that,

despite your best efforts, a certain percentage of your decisions will turn out to be wrong. Give decisions only the time they are worth. Realize that procrastinating on a decision "should be viewed as a decision by default. It's a decision not to decide" (Margaret Spencer Dixon, *When Bad Habits Happen to Good People: How to Rid Yourself of Procrastination and Other Work-Related Vices*).

Then there is the Ben Franklin technique. Ben, the famous eighteenth-century inventor, politician, and philosopher, had a method to help make decisions. Take a piece of paper and fold it in half to make two columns. On one side, list all the reasons for making the decision. On the other side, list all the reasons against making the decision. By comparing these two lists, you can often get clarity on the direction you should go.

> *If I had to sum up in a word what makes a good manager, I'd say decisiveness. You can use the fanciest computers to gather the numbers, but in the end you have to set a timetable and act.*
>
> **—LEE IACOCCA**

I've seen decisive people make the wrong decisions. Interestingly enough, they almost always made the intent of their decisions—that is, their objective—happen anyway. I believe there is some natural law connected with this phenomenon. The act of deciding may, in fact, be more important than the correctness of the actual decision and have more influence on the consequences. Be decisive, take action, and get on with your work and life.

> *A good plan violently executed now is better than a perfect plan executed next week.*
>
> **—GENERAL GEORGE S. PATTON**

## ESTABLISH *DO IT NOW* WORK HABITS

> *Putting off an easy thing makes it hard, and putting off a hard one makes it impossible.*
>
> **—GEORGE H. LORIMER**

Whether we like it or not, we're all creatures of habit. Most of us fall very easily into established routines. How often do you drive the same route to work, or eat at the same restaurant for lunch, or start each workday the same way, for example? Some of these habits and routines are good; others can work against us, and living totally by habit can be very destructive.

Are there habits worth cultivating? Certainly. Habits such as driving safely or showing courtesy to friends and colleagues should be routine and are definitely beneficial. Cultivating the *Do It Now* habit is intended to reinforce an action-oriented lifestyle: to become more decisive and to start and then to stay in motion. Your goal in reading this book is to break your old work habits and to become more efficient, and therefore more productive. Having a decisive and proactive approach toward work will enable you to do exactly that.

Procrastination is itself often only a bad habit.

In his book *Getting Things Done: The ABC's of Time Management* (Scribner, 1976), Edwin Bliss describes procrastination as a habit in this way:

> *When we fail to act as promptly as we should it usually is not because the particular task in question is extremely difficult, but rather because we have formed a habit of procrastinating whenever possible. Procrastination is seldom related to a single item; it is usually an ingrained behavior pattern.*

I couldn't agree more. Learn to *Do It Now* and you'll short-circuit the habit of procrastination. *Do It Now* substitutes an action-oriented behavior for the "do it later" behavior. You act before the mental barriers are activated, so you don't have time to think, "It's too hard; maybe it will go away; maybe someone else will see it; I'm not in the mood; I don't feel like it."

## PERFECTION

Some may believe there is an inherent conflict between *Do It Now* and doing things right. It is good and healthy to expect a high standard of performance. But some people mix up "doing the best possible performance" with when to *act*.

Perfectionists often procrastinate. After all, if you believe you cannot execute the work perfectly, why do it? And *Do It Now* may mean you will not be able to do it as well as you would like.

Dr. Sapadin puts it this way:

*Perfectionists are extreme in their thinking: If they're going to do something, they reason, they should do the best possible job that can be done. There is no acceptable "middle ground."... Faced with a demanding task, perfectionists are inevitably torn between two extremes: giving all they've got, or giving up altogether.*

How can one realistically define that "middle ground"? Should we work to produce that Rolls-Royce, as near to a perfect car as one can get? Or a Mercedes? Or a Ford? The Rolls costs $250,000; the Mercedes, $80,000; the Ford, $25,000. All get you where you want to go. Each auto manufacturer serves a special customer market. That market has a threshold of what its customers are prepared to pay for a car. The manufacturer produces an automobile that meets its customers' expectations.

When acting on your work, don't ask the question of yourself: "What is the best possible job I could do on this task?" Instead ask yourself: "What level or degree of quality do our customers expect from us?" If you have perfectionist tendencies, you are likely to procrastinate; often your customers primarily want you to be responsive.

Certainly, *do it right,* but establish what *right* is and *Do It Now!!*

## DISCIPLINE

A common word heard when discussing the subject of changing behavior is *discipline.* "It is a matter of discipline. If I had more of it, I would be able to exercise,... stop smoking,... diet." While discipline plays a part, I believe it is a red herring. If you exert discipline enough to establish a routine, you make a new habit. The habit helps you maintain the new routine. Discipline yourself to act now, and it will very soon become a habit. Then the habit will lessen the need for discipline. William James, whose studies of human behavior are well known, suggests that if you do something every day for 30 days, it will become a habit. Try it with *Do It Now.*

To be honest, this is more than dealing with procrastination. It is a philosophy toward work and life. It is the view: I am proactive; I am action-oriented; I am bigger than the problems I face. These characteristics begin (and end) with how you face up to and habitually act on the small details of work and life.

So, what is the first thing you should do now? Go ahead—write it down. Focus on the first things. Get yourself organized to *Do It Now,* and do it better!

## FOLLOW-UP FOR CHAPTER 2

**1.** Get started. Go to your desk—if need be, with this book in hand—and go through every single bit and piece of paper on your desk or anywhere near your working space. Pick up the first piece of paper and determine what it is and what must be done to process it to completion. Do whatever is required to complete that task and get that piece of paper off your desk so you never have to look at it again. If a task is going to take you several hours to complete, schedule a time to do it.

**2.** Go through any saved e-mails, voice mails, faxes, and so forth one at a time and begin dealing with each of them to completion. Again, if any will require hours of work, schedule them on your calendar for action at a more appropriate time.

**3.** Determine what tasks ought to be done and decide what must be done to process each task to completion. Take the task as far as you possibly can. If you run into a roadblock, get clever. Ask, "How can I get this done another way?" If you decide to delegate the task or pass it on to someone else, remind yourself to follow-up.

# CHAPTER 3

# Organize It Now!

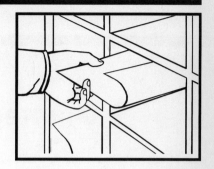

*Don't agonize. Organize.*

—FLORYNCE KENNEDY (FOUNDER, NATIONAL ORGANIZATION FOR
WOMEN—NOW)

# Chapter 3 Preview

In this chapter, you will learn how to:

- Clean up your act and save yourself time.
- Stop wasting your time looking for things. Set up separate file systems for your working papers, reference papers, and archive papers.
- Organize your computer files and set up proper directories for computer files and e-mail.
- Put as much attention to detail in how you are set up to work as you do in the work itself.

You must be well organized to establish the routines that allow you to develop the *Do It Now* habit. You'll be surprised at the time you save just by organizing your work area for maximum efficiency.

## A SOLDIER'S STORY

A soldier is a study in attention to detail. When recruits arrive for basic training at boot camp, they are drilled in what some may consider very fundamental skills. Apart from a tough physical regimen, soldiers are taught in the most forceful way how to make their beds, how to polish their shoes, how to organize their toiletries, how to clean and maintain their weapons, and other fundamentals. The sergeant no doubt wants to impress upon them the need to follow orders. But it is more than that. Basic training in the armed services is just that—basic. Attention to the basics constitutes the foundation for a successful soldier.

There is no more serious profession than that of soldiers, especially during war when their lives are on the line. Considerable thought is put into where a weapon is placed on the body. Soldiers are trained to keep their weapons in meticulous condition. When an enemy is approaching the soldier can't afford to have a gun jam because it wasn't kept clean. Undisciplined, disorganized soldiers who don't know where their weapons are and take no care of them will soon be dead soldiers. That's why sergeants are deadly serious about teaching these basics to new recruits.

How well you are prepared and organized for your work is far more serious than most people recognize. Clutter can be a killer.

> *Clutter and confusion are failures of design, not attributes of information. There's no such thing as information overload.*
> **—EDWARD TUFTE**

## CLEANING OUT THE CLUTTER

Clutter is the mess you face every day when you walk into your office. It's your coat flung over the back of your office guest chair because you didn't hang it on the coat tree that morning. It's the half dozen reports perched on the corner of your filing cabinet and buried under the remains of yesterday's in-office lunch. It's the stack of magazines you haven't gotten around to reading yet. It's the mound of outgoing and incoming mail strewn across your desk. It's the unfinished letters you are writing by hand to give them a personal touch. It's the CD you meant to take home to listen to over the weekend but is now buried under the quarterly budget.

Clutter is the excessive disorganized mess you don't need in your working environment. We may yell at the kids every day to clean up their rooms and then go to a messy office and never even notice anything wrong. But clutter in an office and desk environment prevents us from effectively doing our work.

## WHERE DOES CLUTTER COME FROM?

The first culprit is paper. Whatever happened to the idea of a paperless office? At one time, people speculated that technology would produce an office free of the clutter of paper because everything would be electronic. That still may happen, but it hasn't happened yet. The computer prints out more paper than we can get rid of, and copy machines churn out reams of paper very efficiently. In fact, the flow of paper is probably worse now than it ever was.

E-mail may be even worse than paper clutter, if that's possible. Although e-mail is a wonderful invention, it has created electronic clutter. You can now send a memo to 150 people with a single keystroke. Some people are getting up to 200 e-mail messages a day on a full system. Can you imagine? Or maybe you don't have to.

Then there is stuff. A friend just cleaned out his clothes closet. His wife forced him to do it: She suspected mice were nesting in there. Offices are like clothes closets—places where we accumulate a lot of stuff. The same man and his wife had moved across the street to a new home and taken all their stuff with them. Much of what they moved they had stored months and even years ago in the belief that someday they were going to need it. And they put it all in the storage closet in their new house and ignored it for months.

We laugh about such stories, but they reflect normal behavior. Most people think it is possible they will need all the stuff they keep. Everybody keeps their *National Geographic* magazines, but they never look at them. So why keep them? Why keep them organized? It's like a soldier who would love to carry a tank into battle, but that's just not possible. At some point you have to look realistically at what you're carrying around and make sure you're carrying around things you actually need. If not, get rid of them!


## WHY CLUTTER STAYS THERE

Clutter represents the way people approach both work and life. It tells something about those people—they may have a cluttered mind as well. Many people justify clutter by saying it gives them food for thought and adds to the creative process. Others believe creative and artistic people are just born this way. A colleague of mine once told an interesting story. She described the first time she went to a famous artist's home in New York. Before she went, she had an image in her mind of what a real artist's home would look like: avant-garde, very messy, with paintings stacked in the corners, the studio filled with things to stimulate the creative juices.

But when she walked into his house and looked around, she found that it was neat and tidy. She thought perhaps he'd straightened up since he was expecting guests, but when she found her way into his studio during the evening, she saw that the studio, too, was in perfect order. All the paintbrushes were exactly in order, and the paint cans were neatly lined up and labeled. She could hardly believe what she was seeing—it violated her expectations of how an artist works.

When she asked him about his neatness, he said he had learned it in college, when he had studied art. He had been taught to keep his tools in good working order. He knew that paintbrushes would be ruined unless cleaned after each use. He labeled all the different kinds of paint, because if he didn't, he knew that he'd forget what colors he'd mixed.

If you want to operate effectively, like this artist, you must have things operational and organized. It's simply easier to function in a clean and neat environment.

Some argue that messiness and clutter can be sources of inspiration and creativity. In their book, *A Perfect Mess* (Little, Brown, 2007), authors Eric Abrahamson and David H. Freedman say "moderately disorganized people, institutions, and systems frequently turn out to be more efficient, more resilient, more creative, and in general more effective than highly organized ones." I think the operating word here is "moderately." In addressing clutter, the aim should be the elimination of the unnecessary mess that distracts and prevents you from promptly acting on what you need to act on. The aim is not a "clean" desk. If knickknacks and doodads around your office inspire you, by all means keep them there. But work piled on top of work that gets lost sight of, or that arbitrarily reminds you of things you are not going to do, is not likely to be a source of inspiration. My advice is to avoid extremes in either direction.

## OUT OF SIGHT?

I know people who fear out of sight literally means out of mind. They're afraid they'll forget about a task or an assignment if they don't have some physical reminder of it on their desks or Post-it notes stuck within sight. Keeping everything in sight is their solution.

I agree. Out of sight very often does mean out of mind. When people tell me they have trouble remembering things, I give them a system to remind them. Furthermore, they don't need to be reminded of all the things on their desks that they can't do anything about. Being reminded of what you can't do now only reinforces the bad habit of *Do It Later*.

Although most people who leave assorted paper reminders around the desk and office believe them to be helpful, they are primarily a distraction and mostly just help create stress.

My advice is to create places to put things. Have on your desk only what you are working on, and use a good calendar system to remind yourself to do things when you will, in fact, do them.

## DON'T OVERLOOK THE OBVIOUS

Very often we overlook the obvious in trying to improve the work process. We try to solve more complex problems and miss the fundamentals. The fundamentals a white-collar worker deals with every day include his or her desk, staples, pens, tape, paper clips, lights, file systems, binders, chair, computer, computer disks, and much more. It's not uncommon to walk into an office and find these items in disarray—scissors misplaced, stapler jammed, tape dispenser empty, papers scattered randomly. Yet somehow we expect to work effectively in this condition.

Many people never realize that by not having the basics of their own workplace in order, they handicap themselves from dealing effectively with their day-to-day problems.

Trivial? Maybe, but the *Wall Street Journal* once reported that white-collar workers spend an average of six weeks a year looking for things in the office! Incredible? Yes, but in my experience, true.

I once visited a high-ranking bank executive who was responsible for a region employing 2,500 people. He was a clever businessman who had risen through the ranks due to his leadership ability and business sense. But he was very overloaded and wanted my help sorting it out. One day I noticed a stack of paper on his desk and asked about it. He said it needed to be hole-punched, but he hadn't gotten to it yet. I could have questioned why he was doing it in the first place, but I decided to teach him a lesson on *Do It Now,* and so I asked him to hole-punch it now. He said, "Sure," and proceeded to leave the office. I followed him out past his assistants, down the hall, through a door, down a flight of stairs, and into a supply closet. He took a hole-puncher and walked back to his office and proceeded to punch the holes. Each time he needed to put holes in the paper he went through this process. I asked, "Why not get your own hole-puncher?" He looked at me and said, "What a good idea." He had simply never thought of it.

The obvious isn't only access to the tools you use. Step back and take a good look at your office environment. Is your desk set up most suitably? Is your office warm enough in winter and cool enough in summer? Is your chair comfortable?

Once I did a Personal Efficiency Program (PEP) for Philips Electronics. While visiting one participant's office, I noticed he was very uncomfortable, sitting there and squirming. I asked what the problem was, and he said, "My back hurts."

I examined his chair and saw that it was broken. So I said, "Why don't you get a new chair?"

When I went back for a follow-up visit, he had a new chair. He said, "This is pretty amazing. I got a new chair and my back pain went away. I'm doing so much better at work just because of my new chair."

Another man increased his productivity dramatically simply by having his desk face the window instead of the door. Because the door was open all the time, people walking by would distract him. If he made eye contact, people felt they could stop, come in and say hello, and spend time visiting. As a result, he was constantly interrupted. When he turned his desk and chair so they faced the opposite wall, people stopped interrupting his work.

## START WITH THE BASICS

If you want to organize yourself for greater productivity, you must consider some very basic ideas most people never master. Are your tools operational? Is your product easy to produce? These are two of the questions white-collar workers need to ask themselves, although they rarely do.

On an assembly line, if a worker has to bend over and pick up a heavy tool each time the worker puts a tire on a car, the process needs redesigning. Maybe the worker needs a leverage device of some sort to reduce the time and effort required to put on the tire. Similarly, if you have to rummage through several different papers or directories every time you need to make a phone call, you need to redesign the process. The idea is to make it easy to *Do It Now*.

## YOUR OFFICE TOOLBOX

Let's get specific about the tools you use in your work. If you're not reading this chapter at your desk, imagine yourself there. Think about the physical layout of your work space. What items are there?

1. *Three Trays.* First there should be in, pending, and out baskets or trays for your day-to-day paper flow (not for storage!). Your tray system should look as shown in Figure 3.1.

2. *Standard Office Supplies.* Then there are the things you use every working day: stapler, pens, pencils, scissors, tape, calculator, blank CDs, PDA, Post-it note paper, paper clips, white out, and so forth—all the tools of white-collar work.

I occasionally meet people who have two or three supposedly broken staplers in or on their desks. They're not really broken, of course—they're just jammed, usually because the staples are stuck in the mechanism and no one got around to unsticking them. Worse, each time a stapler was needed the person would borrow one! As insignificant as a stapler may seem, it's a basic tool for a white-collar professional, and having this and other fundamentals in place allows you to work in the most efficient and effective manner.

Make sure that you have all the tools you need and that all of your tools are operational—no more borrowing a pair of scissors or a stapler every time you need one. Take the time to look at all the tools you have or should have. At the end of this little exercise, you will have a stapler, pens, pencils, a pencil sharpener, ruler, ink, toner, scissors,

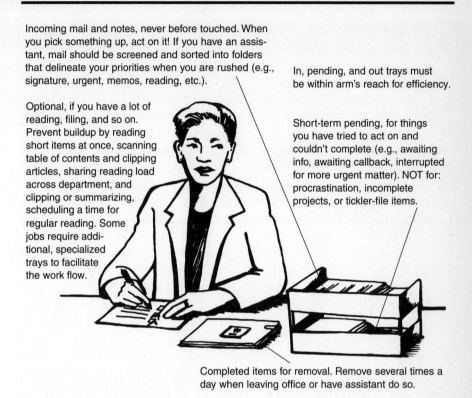

Incoming mail and notes, never before touched. When you pick something up, act on it! If you have an assistant, mail should be screened and sorted into folders that delineate your priorities when you are rushed (e.g., signature, urgent, memos, reading, etc.).

In, pending, and out trays must be within arm's reach for efficiency.

Optional, if you have a lot of reading, filing, and so on. Prevent buildup by reading short items at once, scanning table of contents and clipping articles, sharing reading load across department, and clipping or summarizing, scheduling a time for regular reading. Some jobs require additional, specialized trays to facilitate the work flow.

Short-term pending, for things you have tried to act on and couldn't complete (e.g., awaiting info, awaiting callback, interrupted for more urgent matter). NOT for: procrastination, incomplete projects, or tickler-file items.

Completed items for removal. Remove several times a day when leaving office or have assistant do so.

**Figure 3.1** The tray system.

pads of paper, tape, business card holder, paper clips, staple remover, calculator, blank CDs, flash drives, files, file labels, and whatever other items you normally use in the course of a day, and they should all be fully functional. These routine items should be stored in the middle drawer of your desk or in the shallower side drawers of the desk—not on your work surface.

At the same time, be alert to waste. I often hear stories of incredible waste from the accounting departments of companies. People say, "Once we got organized, we found what we had in inventory, what we were using and wasting." When calculated, the amount of waste often boggles the mind.

I once taught PEP to a medium-size brokerage firm. I started going through desks one by one. I told people, "Make sure to gather up any extra supplies you have, so they can be returned to central supply." I do this because people often complain that they go to central supply but can't find what they need or, in small companies, that the supply budget has been spent for the quarter or the year, and there's no money to buy additional supplies. Well, as I went through PEP with about 120 people in the company, I rounded up all the extra supplies people had in their desks. In the end there were enough supplies to last a year without buying a single thing! All that was needed was to organize what we'd retrieved from everyone's desks. And that's typical. If you're up to the challenge, look in, on, and around your own desk. I bet you'll find half a dozen extra pens and other supplies you didn't even know you had.

The same principle that applies to supplies in your desk also applies to information in your files: *You don't use what you don't realize you have.* And without organization and maintenance, you don't realize what you have. You're wasting resources. Think of the survivors of a shipwreck, on the ocean in a rubber raft. The first thing they have to do is account, item by item, for every resource available to them so nothing is wasted. Waste in such a situation could cost them their lives.

## BECOME FAMILIAR WITH TOOLS AS THEY COME ON THE MARKET

Keep up with the best time management systems and tools. Make a habit of browsing through catalogs or at an office supply store periodically to discover new resources and tools. You may be surprised at what you find.

I recall one woman who worked for an insurance company. She was very disorganized and didn't want to follow my suggestions. It so happened she had a unique job and my solutions didn't exactly match her circumstances. But then one day a colleague brought in a time management system that employed three-by-five-inch cards and a leather binder with little sleeves to hold the cards. The system required users to write a task on each card, and to slip the card for any task not completed into a sleeve for the next day. Well, the colleague found this system useless but rather than throw it away she gave it to this woman, who loved it and ended up solving many problems by using it.

Many excellent tools can be employed to increase both your effectiveness and your efficiency. One person may find one tool ineffective whereas another person can't live without it. Take advantage of the tools that exist and find tools that are suited to your style and personality.

## ORGANIZING FILES—BEGINNING WITH PAPER

Although many of us are evolving from a paper-based system to electronic documents, a tremendous amount of paper still needs to be dealt with by most of us. Whether you have lots or little, we have found that by first addressing the paper, the rest of the organizing process becomes easier and faster. If you have little in the way of paper to deal with, you can skip this section and move on to Organizing Electronic Files on page 58.

To deal better with paperwork, organize your papers and files by frequency of use. The things you use most frequently need to be near at hand. Your desk is a work surface, and the only papers on it should be those you are working with currently.

Figure 3.2, showing paper control points, gives an overview of good office organization.

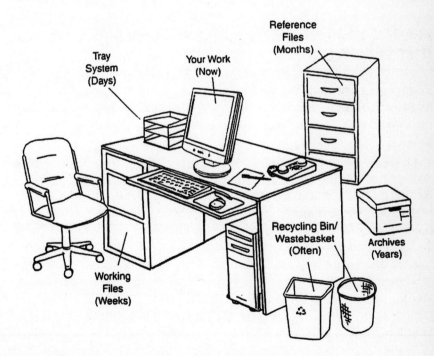

**Figure 3.2**   Paper control points.

You should have a three-basket system for handling paper flow. Figure 3.1 illustrates how the tray system might look and how it would be best used. Your in, pending, and out baskets (trays) are for tasks completed over the course of a few days at most. Next set up three types of files: working files, reference files, and archive files. These three files are vital paper control points for managing your work flow.

1. *Working files* are for current projects and routine functions. Usually 80% of your work involves 20% of your files, so these files should be kept within arm's reach, most likely in your desk drawers as hanging files. Working files are for items you're concerned with regularly over several weeks or months and for ongoing projects you're responsible for.
2. *Reference files* contain the bulk of the files in your office. Since you use your reference files regularly they need to be near you, but not necessarily within arm's reach.
3. *Archive files* are kept for statutory reasons and may rarely be needed. They represent the accumulated work of past years and may be stored outside the office.

## Working Files

Once a man who kept five tall piles of paper on his desk told me with a straight face that he knew exactly where everything was. I asked, "Then you don't think there's any value in having a system?" He gestured to the mess on his desk and answered: "I have a system. This is my system."

Then the telephone rang. The caller asked him to refer to a memo sent out a few days before. "Yeah, sure, one second," he said in response to this request. He went to a pile and leafed through it; then to another pile and leafed through it; then he looked at me sheepishly, his face turning red, and went to yet another pile. Embarrassed, he told the caller, "I'll have to get back to you."

I just sat there and looked at him. Then he said: "Well, maybe there is a need for a file system, but honestly, that missing paper was right next to the blue piece of paper in that folder."

People think they know where things are, but they waste precious time looking because they really *don't* know. It would be unreasonable to expect them to remember where every single piece of paper is.

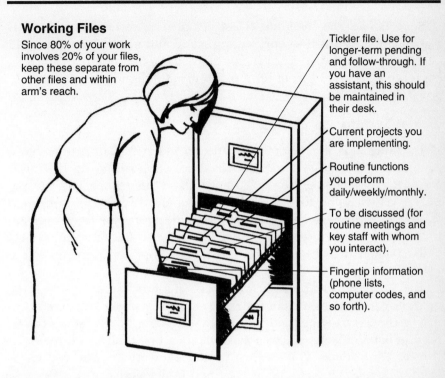

### Working Files

Since 80% of your work involves 20% of your files, keep these separate from other files and within arm's reach.

Tickler file. Use for longer-term pending and follow-through. If you have an assistant, this should be maintained in their desk.

Current projects you are implementing.

Routine functions you perform daily/weekly/monthly.

To be discussed (for routine meetings and key staff with whom you interact).

Fingertip information (phone lists, computer codes, and so forth).

**Figure 3.3** Working files.

That's what your working files are for. As shown in Figure 3.3, working files usually contain several types of information:

1. *Fingertip Information.* These files contain phone lists, address lists, computer codes, company policies, and other information you refer to frequently and want at your fingertips when you need it.
2. *Items "To Be Discussed."* Create a file for routine meetings and a file for each staff member with whom you interact.
3. *Routine Functions.* These files contain information that you need for routine tasks performed daily, weekly, or monthly.
4. *Current Projects.* These are the projects you're working on now. Create a hanging file for each project and include anything necessary for your current work. Clean out these files now and then move certain less urgent items to your reference files.

5. *A Tickler File.* This file is usually divided in two parts: One is numbered 1 to 12, representing the months of the year; the other part is numbered 1 to 31, for the days of the month. The tickler file is used for longer-term pending and follow-through items.

## Tickler System

By creating a tickler file system and checking it daily, you have a foolproof reminder system. For example, suppose we're scheduled to meet on December 15. You might place the agenda and the papers you will bring to the meeting under the 15. Also in your tickler file at appropriate points throughout the month of December are items such as "Verify flight schedule" and "Check Chicago connection," along with a note to remind you to brief your replacement before your trip.

The tickler file can be used for storage in a way that avoids clogging up your pending basket. For instance, suppose you have an agreement that you need to write, and you know it's going to take some hours. So you have all sorts of papers—perhaps a first draft to be rewritten by a given deadline. You haven't done this rewrite because you know from experience it will take at least two hours, and you don't have a two-hour block to devote to it until Thursday. So you block out two hours on Thursday's calendar, and you place the rough report in the tickler file for Thursday, the eleventh under the 11, where you know you'll find it when you're ready to get down to work. Then, because it's your habit to check the tickler file each morning, on the eleventh you locate the rough draft in your file and check your calendar. Sure enough, you've blocked out time between 9 and 11 AM to work on the report. And when the final draft is completed, you'll place it in your out basket and route it to the next person involved.

Everything I am referring to in a paper tickler system applies equally to an electronic tickler system. It can be a specific personal information manager (PIM) software, or a personal digital assistant (PDA) like the popular Palm Pilot. Such electronic tickler systems often exist as part of an e-mail system. For those of us without administrative support, electronic systems are often more effective and easier to use than paper-based systems.

You can see why it's essential to check the tickler file daily. This is the essence of the *Do It Now* philosophy. After checking the tickler file for the day, you know exactly what you must do to keep on schedule and accomplish the tasks that will move you further along in your work.

## Setting Up Your Personal Working Files

It is vital to develop a file structure that embraces all your work, is easy to conceptualize, and, most important, facilitates the retrieval of the information you need. When this is done, it is easy to decide where to file a document and where to look for it when you need to retrieve it—whether it is a working, reference, or archive file. You need to create specific files to have a workable system. You do this by mapping out your key responsibilities and the activities and information required to accomplish these tasks. See Figure 3.4 for an idea of the responsibilities a plant manager might list.

This is a simplified job-analysis process. List the broad categories of responsibilities you have as key words. Usually there are about six to eight key responsibilities that comprise your job. Then list subcategories for these broader responsibilities. Use the form found in Figure 3.5 to help identify and label files representing the important parts of your work.

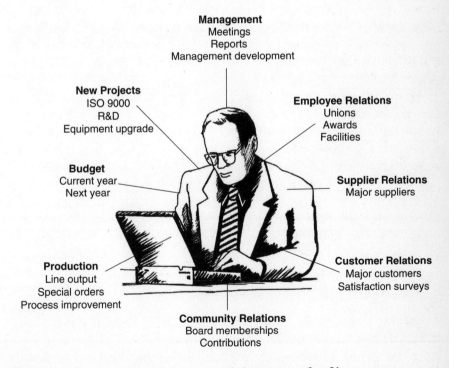

**Management**
Meetings
Reports
Management development

**New Projects**
ISO 9000
R&D
Equipment upgrade

**Employee Relations**
Unions
Awards
Facilities

**Budget**
Current year
Next year

**Supplier Relations**
Major suppliers

**Production**
Line output
Special orders
Process improvement

**Customer Relations**
Major customers
Satisfaction surveys

**Community Relations**
Board memberships
Contributions

**Figure 3.4** Example of a responsibilities map for files structure.

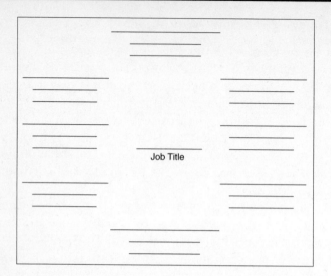

**Figure 3.5**   Sample responsibilities mapping form.

As you set up your own working files, follow these guidelines:

1. *Select your working files drawer,* most likely one of your larger desk drawers. Remember, this is information you want close at hand. Label the drawer appropriately and clearly in big, bold letters.
2. *Remove all nonworking files.* Move them to either reference files or archive files.
3. *Make sure you have a file folder for each project and activity.* Label each file appropriately and clearly.
4. *Set up a tickler file.* One part is numbered 1 to 12, representing the months of the year, the other part of the tickler file is numbered 1 to 31, for the days of the month.
5. *Remove files that are no longer active.* Move them to either reference files or archive files.

## Your Personal Reference Files: Note Things to Do as You Come across Them

As you are going through this sort, purge, and organize process, you will likely notice some tasks you need to do. You should write these tasks down immediately. David Allen, in his excellent book *Getting Things Done* (Penguin Books, 2001), refers to this as "capturing" all the things to be done: "Anything you consider unfinished in any way must be captured in a trusted system outside your mind, or in what I call a 'collection bucket,' that you know you'll come back to regularly and sort through."

You will need to make a decision about where these tasks should be noted—the system you will use to manage your things to do. Although I am not a big fan of Microsoft Outlook, most companies use it (or Lotus Notes) for managing e-mail. Consolidating all of your e-mail, contacts, tasks, calendar, and notes in one place is the best way to manage your work. With Microsoft Outlook or Lotus Notes you can categorize and organize your to-dos, drag things to do into your calendar for scheduled work, and set electronic reminders. Again, I am not advocating any particular software application. But I do believe if you are currently using a paper-based system you can make big strides in your personal efficiency by converting to an electronic equivalent.

One more important point: The to-do you write down should express the specific next step. It is not "buy a home." That would be too broad. When you see a to-do like this, you have to figure out the action you must take. A better action item might be "call John (your mortgage loan officer) and set an appointment to review household finances, to determine the mortgage I can afford." Figure out the action (next step) immediately and only once. Note the next step in your planning tool, so that when you are ready to act, you will know exactly what to do.

You're now going to create your own reference files. Your reference files will contain these items:

- Research for your future projects.
- Past projects to which you refer.
- Resource information.
- Personnel information.
- Administrative data.
- Budget information.
- Client account records.

As you set up your reference files, consider these two things:

1. What information do you have to keep?
2. How can you best organize your reference files for ease of retrieval?

**Reference Files Structure**

To efficiently locate a file in reference files containing several drawers or cabinets, a simple alphabetical arrangement is usually inadequate, and subject categories must be established. A position can be broken down into key functions, which should be reflected in your file categories.

**Reference File Cabinet**

**Reference File Drawer**

ADMINISTRATIVE

GOVT. CONTRACTS

NON-GOVT. CONTRACTS

TRADE FAIRS

**Figure 3.6** Reference files structure.

The following ideas might help you to structure your reference files (see Figure 3.6):

1. List the key components of your job (e.g., contracts, trade fairs, product development, budget, personnel). These will become the categories in your reference files.
2. Label file folders clearly and appropriately, based on the categories you identified.
3. Cull existing files and throw away useless paper.
4. Using hanging files, organize drawers with one or more categories.
5. Alphabetize files within categories or subcategories.
6. Label file drawers and file folders with large, clear letters to make retrieval and refiling easier and faster.

## Archive Files

Archive files are most often set up for common use, so how they are structured and categorized may be different from how you might choose to set up your personal files. There may, in fact, be two systems required: an individual one in your office for archival documents related strictly to your job, and a second system outside your office for common use.

At one company, I found in a file drawer a memo dated 1906. No one had gone through those files since 1906! The memo was on how to clean the office. True. One of our PEP consultants carried a little case with screwdrivers and a hammer because it was so common to go into offices and find that some of the cabinets couldn't even be opened.

Staff members are generally reluctant to use the archive system because they feel they can't trust it. Management's responsibility is to provide a functional archive system; staff's responsibility is to understand the archive system and use it correctly.

The following questions will give you an indication of the state of your archive file system:

- Do you have departmental archives? What about company archives?
- What is the policy on document retention?
- Who is responsible for maintaining archives?
- Does an indexing system exist?
- What are the procedures for retrieving documents from archives?
- Can you rely on documents being recovered if needed?
- Have you tested this system lately?
- Do archive files need to be implemented? If so, who should do this?

I find that no matter how complete a departmental archive system might be, there's almost always a need for some form of personal archive system in the office. The personal archives can reside in the cabinets furthest away from the desk, since they will be the least-referenced files.

## TIPS—WHAT TO KEEP, WHERE TO KEEP IT, AND WHAT TO THROW AWAY

For many people, throwing things away is difficult. Just how much information should you retain? Consider the following:

- Do you tend to hold onto things "just in case"?
- Do you keep too much in your reference files?

- When deciding whether to save something, take Stephanie Winston's advice from her book *Getting Organized* (Warner Books, 1991) and ask yourself, "If I needed this again, where can I get it?"
- Does a copy already exist in electronic form?
- Can someone else in the organization provide the information? If so, don't duplicate his or her files unless you use this information frequently.
- Should any of these working, reference, and archive files be kept in a common departmental reference file system?
- Do you need to coordinate with anyone to determine who will save certain pieces of information?
- Do you need to coordinate with anyone with whom you share reference files on how you will organize files?

## TIPS FOR IMPROVING YOUR PAPER FILING SYSTEM

The following suggestions (see also Figure 3.7) will make your filing system more efficient:

- Use hanging files. Hanging files support folders better and facilitate refiling in the correct place. Box-bottom hanging files can hold several manila folders on the same subject.
- Label files with large, clear letters. This facilitates retrieval and refiling.
- Align category labels and subcategory labels. Aligning the tabs according to categories and subcategories allows the eye to scan to the correct file more efficiently. Categories can be given colored labels to further aid scanning. (Make sure this step is necessary and useful. I was told of one secretary who spent an entire day color coding her supervisor's files only to discover he was color-blind.)
- Create an index for large reference files. This index enables anyone to retrieve files easily in the secretary's absence. It also minimizes duplicate files and coordinates the use of shared files.

## FILING AND LABELING

The main purpose in filing anything is to be able to find it again. The easiest way to do this is to create broad, general categories that will

**Filing Tips**

❏ **Use hanging files.**

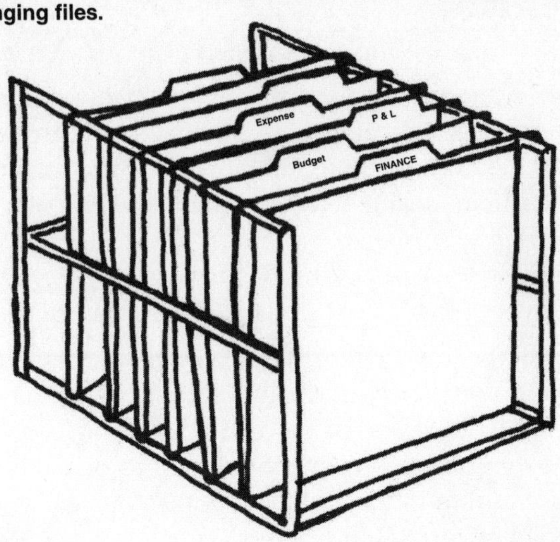

❏ **Label with large, clear letters.**

❏ **Align category and subcategory labels.**

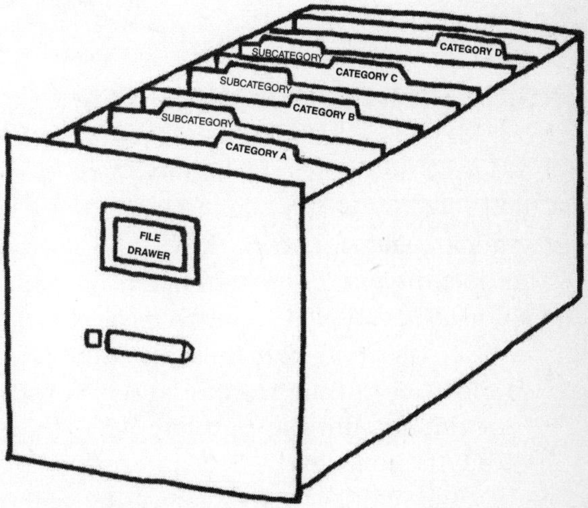

❏ **Create an index for large reference files for manager's use.**

**Figure 3.7**  Filing tips.

be genuinely useful and easily understood by others. A good rule of thumb is to set up file systems not only so you can find things, but also so anyone else can find them. The reason is twofold: (1) on occasion somebody else may need to find items in your files, and (2) if it's simple enough for someone else to use, it's probably simple enough for you. You can always subcategorize within a broad category, but the main idea is to have bigger categories. Label your drawers as well as the files within them, using lettering that is big, bold, and easy to read.

---

*Tip:* If you create a new system, you may have a hard time re-membering where you placed a document later. You may not be used to the new file locations or the categories you have created yet. Because most papers represent something to do in the future, you should make a note in the task to remind yourself where you have placed the papers for future reference.

---

## ORGANIZING ELECTRONIC FILES

Not too long ago you only had to worry about paper (as if that wasn't enough!). Today most of us depend more on the documents in our computers to get our work done than we do the paper on our desks. Digital documents can include letters, e-mail, web pages, spreadsheets, and so on. Because it is so much easier to create digital documents and they are for the most part invisible, they tend to proliferate more than paper. Since electronic storage space is relatively cheap, it is easy to save documents. But the problem isn't storing and saving documents; it's finding them again.

Fortunately, advances in technology are making finding files easier. It wasn't always that way. Those of us who began using computers with MS-DOS (Microsoft Disk Operating System) remember how difficult it was to organize the documents on the hard drive. The biggest single barrier was probably DOS's eight-letter naming convention. As a result of DOS limiting the number of characters one could use in a file name to eight, you would find files named 4Q99cshf.wk3 (which meant, in real life, fourth-quarter cash flow spreadsheet)—hard to decipher and harder yet to remember.

Technology has made it easier to find documents by providing more than one place to easily file (or copy) the same document and more than one way to locate a document.

When you organize your computer documents with the following points in mind, you will waste little time finding what you need to get the job done.

A computer is much like an empty filing cabinet. You can dump your data files into it in a pile, or you can group your applications and files, set up general categories, divide them into drawers, and subcategorize the files in these drawers, much as you would with your paper files. It is possible, and desirable, to organize the hard drive, the desktop (a term used in Windows describing the background where the graphic symbols called objects or icons reside), menus (the list of options and/or instructions to be found by clicking on an icon or object), and files (electronic documents that have been given a name and stored on your computer).

The recommended process for organizing the computer and its electronic files is to:

1. Create a file system for the document files in the computer.
2. Create a file system for retained e-mail messages.
3. Have the system mirror the organization of the rest of your information (paper and electronic).
4. Transfer those documents you wish to retain into their appropriate electronic folders.
5. Create a computer desktop that makes access to files and applications easy.

## Where to Begin—The Computer's Operating System

It is through the operating system on the computer (be it any version of Windows, Mac, or another operating system) that application and document files can be found. Each operating system has its own set of commands or icons that allow you to manipulate files and organize them for easy use. The first step toward organizing your computer information is to get a working knowledge of your operating system file management protocol. Run through the tutorial. Search out file management in the "help" section and study up. If you are like me—lost, slow to learn, and possessing modest skills in only one language (English, nontechnical!)—you might seek out a computer coach (someone technically skilled with a working knowledge of your operating system) to coach you through the learning process. In large organizations seek help from your information systems department or a knowledgeable administrative support person. The rule is: Before you start messing with your computer files, know what you are doing or find someone who does.

## Back Up Your Hard Drive

No matter how skilled you may be with file management, it is wise to do a complete backup (make a copy) of your hard drive before you begin deleting and reorganizing your files. In later versions of Windows, it is as simple as going into Microsoft Tools in the Start and Programs menu, selecting Backup, and following the instructions. You no doubt have a method of backing up your computer files. Whether you do it regularly enough is something to consider. If you do not do it at all, you are setting yourself up for big problems in the future. Regardless, be certain to back up your files before you take on the following.

---

***Tip:*** If possible, consider backing up the whole hard drive, including applications, on an external drive. It is always prudent to back up your data files. But in the case of a crashed and nonrecoverable hard drive, it can be a huge task reinstalling programs.

---

## Naming Electronic Files

The design of your computer file system should mirror your paper file system.

A typical computer user might have the following documents to organize:

- Word processing documents.
- Spreadsheet documents.
- Saved e-mail messages.
- Documents downloaded and saved from the Internet.
- Groupware databases.
- Personal finance files (like Quicken).
- Project planning files.

- Photos.
- PowerPoint presentation files.
- And so on.

Use your paper system file names to help create your electronic document file categories. The simplest way would be to make a list of the names of your paper files in your working, reference, and archive cabinets/drawers. How to create file names on your computer and how to manipulate these files (move them from one location to another) depend on the operating system you use.

Using the appropriate operating system commands, do the following:

1. Create a My Documents folder (if not already on your C: drive). Create three subfolders (directories) under My Documents. Name them 1Working, 2Reference, and 3Archive. Working, reference, and archive electronic file categories allow you to store your document files in a system identical to your paper files. Putting the numeral "1" next to the name of your most important file directory (working) will position it at the top of the My Documents tree. The numeral "2" places the reference files below the working directory, and the numeral "3" puts the archive files below the reference directory.

2. Using your prepared list of paper files, create a matching set of subfolders (subdirectories) in the 1Working, 2Reference, and 3Archive electronic directories. (See Figure 3.8.) The end result of creating these directories and subdirectories might look like Figure 3.9.

3. Now that you have named your electronic file directories you can go through the electronic document files of each of your software applications and transfer your documents into their appropriate folders (directories). You should have three main objectives in going through document files of your computer. These would be to:

- Purge unnecessary files. (If you are uncertain whether to eliminate the document, then don't. It is better to keep it than to delete it and later find out you needed it.)
- Rename, as may be necessary, any document files you keep.
- Place the document files in the appropriate 1Working, 2Reference, and 3Archive directories.

| First Tier | Second Tier | Third Tier | Fourth Tier |
|---|---|---|---|
| **Main file folder/directory structure** These folders/ directories are set up using numbers as the first character to ensure their placement at the top of the hard disk tree structure. | **Responsibilities** This folder/ directory tier should be general headings resulting from the responsibility map and will not contain specific files. | **Specific names of subdirectories** The names chosen for subdirectories must be general in nature with each tier giving more information about the files in the grouping. When the number of files in a group becomes excessive, start thinking about creating further subdirectories of the existing group. | **Files** Careful thought is necessary when choosing a file name. Use only abbreviations that are meaningful to you and instantly recognizable. Be consistent with your format and name files so that you will have some idea what it is if you see it away from its home folder/ directory. |
| Working files *(folder or folder/ directory)* **1Working** | **Clients Customers Finances Forms People (Personnel) Pending Projects (etc.)** | Actual client/ customer names Expense record, budgets Form names or numbers Actual names of people or personnel records Items awaiting completion Projects currently in progress | |
| Reference files *(folder or directory)* **2Reference** | **Graphs/Charts Spreadsheets Completed projects Expense reports Reports Evaluations (etc.)** | | |
| Archive files *(folder or directory)* **3Archive** | **Previous year's tax returns "Must saves"** | | |

**Figure 3.8**  Organizing your hard drive with Windows Explorer.

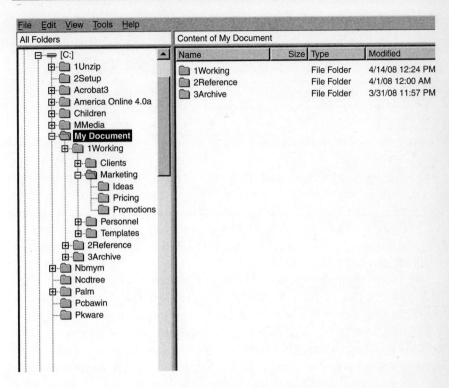

**Figure 3.9**   How the file directories might look on your computer.

## LET THE COMPUTER FIND YOUR DOCUMENTS FOR YOU

I have given you a rather lengthy way to organize your electronic documents for easier retrieval. I believe it is useful to devote the time to such a process. The process disciplines you in naming protocols, purges out old and useless files, and helps you identify resources you may forget you even have.

You have a resource now, and if you take the time to learn it, you will find retrieving documents can be a snap. That is your computer's "Search" function. Scores of add-on software resources can make searching for documents easier. See the section on Using Search Functions later on in this chapter for more information on search tools.

## ORGANIZING E-MAIL

It is not uncommon to find people receiving upwards of 200 e-mail messages a day. Obviously, this can be overwhelming. To process this mail in an efficient and effective way is the subject of a later chapter. How to organize the e-mail messages you keep so as to be able to easily find them again is the topic of this section.

Like your paper in basket, the electronic mailbox can fill up quickly. Some systems allow hundreds of messages to accumulate in the inbox. This can become unmanageable and cause slowdowns. One of the most important buttons on the keyboard is the delete key. Obviously, the more you delete, the less you need to organize and file. Nevertheless, there will be e-mail messages you will need to keep. Messages you do keep should be stored in the correct computer directory or electronic folder.

Many e-mail applications allow you to create electronic storage folders for those messages you need to keep but do not want to leave in the same location as your incoming e-mail. Which messages you want to keep or delete will depend on the company policy regarding retention of e-mail. Recent developments in which large companies have found themselves in a legal nightmare because they have retained e-mail messages (or haven't for that matter) tell you that this topic is very important. Ninety percent of all major corporations have e-mail and document retention policies. Unfortunately, most staff members have never been trained on these policies, are unaware, and don't follow them. Before you decide to delete anything, make sure that you are in compliance with corporate policy.

Once you have determined what you need to keep and what you don't need to keep, it is a matter of setting up an organizational structure that allows you to easily find e-mail messages that have been stored.

The easiest way to begin this process is to use the responsibility map designed for your paper-based system to create folders of the same name in your e-mail application.

Apart from any other e-mail storage folders you may want to create, I advise you to create a folder called "Pending/Follow-up." In this folder you place e-mail messages received or sent requiring some form of input from elsewhere or needing to be followed through by you. This is an excellent way to remove and store messages that would otherwise remain in the inbox and remain a distraction. The most important thing to remember about this "Pending/Follow-up" folder is to routinely check it to make sure that you do in fact follow through on messages that have been placed there.

## Steps to Organize E-Mail

1. Begin by identifying your e-mail file features. Using the Help function, determine how to set up a folder system within your particular e-mail application.
2. Using your responsibility map and categories created for your paperwork file system, set up a mirrored system of categories within your e-mail application.
3. In the process of going through your e-mail one at a time, identify whether you should:

   • Delete it.
   • File it on either your personal C: drive, personal server drive (should it exist), or shared drive on the server.

4. If transferring the file to your shared drive, verify that the name of the file is intuitive and will make it possible for you to easily find it again.
5. Go through your e-mail messages one by one and follow this process until complete.
6. If you are beginning this process with a large backlog of unorganized e-mail, you may wish simply to set up the folder organization, choose a cutoff date for these earlier documents (like the beginning of the year), create an archive folder, transfer these documents en masse to it, and forget about them. If you need to look up an older message, you can do so by accessing the archive folder and then reclassifying it in the new folder structure. (See Figure 3.10.)

## CREATING AND ORGANIZING YOUR E-MAIL ADDRESS BOOK

Your e-mail application memorizes e-mail addresses, and these can be put into an e-mail address book. Most e-mail applications organize the addresses in alphabetical order, but it is possible to create general categories (groupings) within the address book list and file addresses under these general groupings.

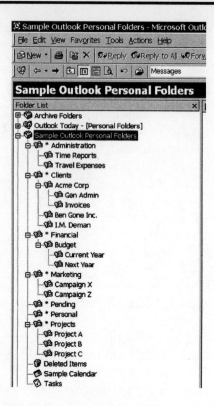

**Figure 3.10** E-mail folder organization.

For example, I organize my address book by group according to those who work in my business, those who are clients, and, under the grouping/category "Personal," family and friends. The number of e-mail addresses I have determines how specific I might be in both organizing and grouping the addresses. I wouldn't organize lots of groupings if I had only a few e-mail addresses.

Not only does organizing e-mail addresses according to groups make it easier to find the address I'm looking for, it also allows me to send specific e-mails more easily to the members of the group.

## ORGANIZING BOOKMARKS—WEB PAGES YOU MAY WISH TO ACCESS IN THE FUTURE

If you use the Internet often, you might wish to have access to useful web pages again in the future. One simple tool offered by nearly all Internet browsers is bookmarks or Favorites. Assign the page to

Favorites. You can categorize and organize the web page for future reference, an easy process that should be done.

You can take this a step further and sign up for Delicious services (http://delicious.com) and "tag" the web page. Tags are labels you can assign to pages, photos, videos, articles, and so on, on the Internet. To use tags, you "tag" (name) and save a link to a personal area of Delicious. Delicious adds the link with the same tag where others can see it. Anyone can look up the tag and see all entries. Others may want to add a different tag name, and if so, Delicious adds the tags for all to see.

It is another way of organizing and finding information online, but with the benefit of seeing many more web pages of interest that others have collected on the tag topic.

## ORGANIZING THE COMPUTER DESKTOP TO ACCESS APPLICATIONS AND FILES EASILY

The computer desktop is that screen you see when you first turn on your computer. It is the electronic equivalent of the top surface of the desk in your office. The computer desktop can be organized much in the same way you would organize and utilize your office desk. The documents, electronic files, and ongoing projects that you access most frequently can be placed and organized on the computer desktop.

For instance, most Windows programs allow you to create categories of and group software applications so you can easily access these applications on your computer desktop. A group for "Finance Programs" might include Quicken for personal finance, Lotus 1-2-3 for spreadsheet work, and QuickBooks for business accounts.

Often accessed documents can be grouped and named, and an icon placed on the desktop. You can simply click the icon, the software program is launched, and up pops the document.

It is worth the effort to study how to organize the desktop for your operating system and how to set up the desktop for easy access to files and applications.

## USING SEARCH FUNCTIONS

You can avoid this whole reorganizing process and use the improved search functions found in the newest of operating systems and other applications. Google and Yahoo have desktop search applications modeled after their popular search engines. If you do not have the time or inclination to go through your electronic files, this may be a good option for you. Refamilarizing yourself with the documents on your computer is a healthy exercise for anyone. It is not uncommon to find that you have many resources you have forgotten about. If you know where something is and can find it by following a logical path, you do not need to search through a long list of similar documents. And, although the newest of Search applications are fast and accurate, there are some downsides to completely depending on them.

I am not enamored with Microsoft's Find function. The search takes too long. That said, it does have the advantage of sorting the results in more ways than you find with Google or Yahoo desktop searches.

Google Desktop and Yahoo's X1 Professional Client are much faster. According to their own literature, they begin (as all search applications do) by indexing all documents and files. Both automatically index new documents as they are created or downloaded. Once indexed, both provide full text searches over your e-mail, files, music, photos, chats, web pages, and so on.

Google Desktop search results' page lists all the items in your index that match your search terms. By default, it orders the results by when you last saw each item. It has limited sort functionality (by relevance and date). Google has a nifty shortcut to open a search—hit control two times and a search box opens up.

Yahoo's X1 Professional Client operates much the same, but has a few more sort options, including searches by name, date, document type, size, and file location.

The latest versions of Microsoft Outlook and Lotus Notes have improved search functions. Whether you have "organized" your e-mail folders and categorized your tasks or not, you should familiarize yourself with them.

One final thought. Whether you go through the process of organizing your electronic documents, choose to take the "search" route, or use a combination of both, stay alert to the pitfalls and remember to tweak your system so it becomes easier and easier for you to act. That is the outcome you really want.

## ORGANIZING OTHER MEDIA

Other items that might need to be organized include books, shelves, briefcase, address book, business cards, and floppy disks. See Figure 3.11 for guidance.

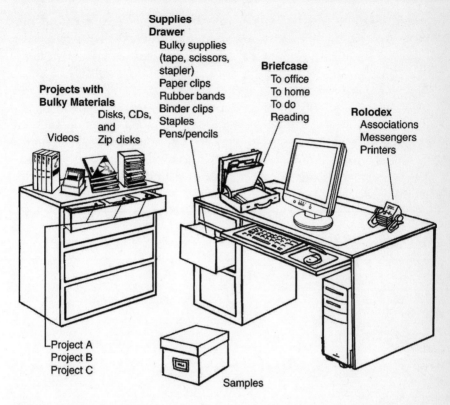

**Figure 3.11** Adapting the principles of organizing to other media.

The rules of thumb for organizing these other media are:

- Group similar things together.
- Place them in their own space or container.
- Label them clearly.

Supplies such as paper clips, pens, Post-it notes, thumbtacks, and stamps can be organized in desk drawers using specially designed plastic trays to hold and separate the supplies.

Even the automobile may need to be organized if you spend lots of time traveling to and from customers!

## SUMMARY

It isn't easy to get organized. After all, it can be boring, tedious work. And like most boring tasks, you might prefer to put it off for another time.

When our PEP trainers deliver our PEP service we often find ourselves acting as the catalyst—encouraging the participants to get on with it. But we likely won't be there when you get ready to start; it will be up to you to do it. Try to keep in mind that you will have a much easier time getting work done as a result.

The more thoroughly you do the program, the more you will get out of it. I often ask my course participants how much attention to detail they place on, say, a sales presentation. "Oh, lots!" they say. I suggest they give the same attention to detail to how they organize themselves as they would to a special presentation. Do the same! You will not be disappointed.

## FOLLOW-UP FOR CHAPTER 3

**1.** Clear the backlog and organize your work area. Very likely you will require a day or more to do this. If at all possible, schedule this time so you work undisturbed.

**2.** Get at least three trays and mark them "In," "Pending," and "Out." Your in basket will receive all new material. Your pending basket is for those things you cannot do now, for things that are out of your control. Your out basket is for all those papers you've completed.

**3.** Begin by emptying the drawer that will become your "working file" or "active drawer" so you can create organized files there. (On subsequent days, you can schedule in your calendar to continue the process with your reference file drawers.) Continue the process of emptying everything from your drawers, file cabinets, paper trays, walls, briefcase, and so on, every piece of paper and placing them onto your desk. Look everywhere: under the blotter, behind the curtain, under the desk. Gather all of your papers and pile them indiscriminately on top of your desk.

**4.** Pick up the top piece of paper and deal with it now in one of the following ways:

- Deal with it until completed.
- Deal with it as completely as you can and then place it in the pending basket if very short-term or the tickler file under the appropriate date while awaiting a response.

- Delegate it.
- Create a pile on the floor for papers needed for ongoing work or projects to file in your working files.
- Create another pile on the floor for papers to file in the reference file, if it's information you need but which requires you to do nothing at the moment.
- Create a pile on the floor for papers to file in the archive file.
- Throw it away! Do this if it's trivial, of no use, already dealt with, or exists elsewhere.

**5.** Using the responsibility map (see Figure 3.4) begin identifying where the saved documents go.

**6.** After all this, set up your working files. Create hanging files and labels for each work project and general category. Create files and labels for the reference files and archive files.

**7.** Create individual follow-up files for each of your subordinates and your boss or peers with whom you have regular contact. Label each file with the person's name, and place in that file notes about things you need to check on regarding ongoing, long-term projects.

**8.** If you still use lots of paper in your work, consider creating a tickler file to organize the papers you need to follow through on at a specific time or date. If you mainly work in an electronic environment, make a point of setting reminders in the system you use to track tasks, or use the calendar to set reminders. You want to use your system to assist you in remembering, and not depend solely on your memory.

**9.** Organize your e-mail inbox. Your aim is an empty inbox, with all of the e-mails you are retaining organized into folders in the inbox folder tree. Clearing e-mails works best if you work from the bottom up, starting with the oldest e-mails first. First, learn your e-mail application file features. Use your responsibility map to identify folder categories. Go through all of your inbox e-mail and either respond, delegate, task it (if it is something to do in the future), or discard it—for every e-mail, either file it to a folder or delete it.

**10.** If your documents are on the C: drive, create 1Working, 2Reference, and 3Archive folders for your saved electronic documents.

**11.** Using the responsibility map begin creating a set of subfolders that mirror your paper file system and represent the key categories you will set up within your electronic file system.

**12.** Begin the process of reviewing all of your stored electronic documents. Decide:

- Is this a document you use or will use?
- Can it be accessed elsewhere?
- If you are to keep it, where should it be stored?
- Should the file be renamed?
- Should the file be deleted?
- Act on your decisions.

**13.** If you do not have the time or inclination to go through your electronic files, as in 9 through 12, then my advice is for you to learn your Microsoft Outlook or Lotus Notes search functions, look into improved search applications like Google Desktop, Yahoo X1 Professional Client, or another third-party application, and then test and get adept enough with them so that you can find your electronic documents rapidly.

**14.** If you do not have the time to set aside a day or two for this process, follow Julie Morgenstern's advice in *Never Check E-Mail in the Morning* (Simon & Schuster, 2004), and target the areas that need fixing. Break up the organizing project according to what the obvious needs are, and clean up one area at a time. As you complete one area, you can switch back to your normal work, picking up one more area at a time when it is convenient to you.

**15.** Make a list of missing supplies and tools necessary for you to do your job: pen, tape, staples, scissors, envelopes, stamps, extra file folders, labels, formatted disks, and anything else you may need. Make sure you have them all on hand and that everything works.

That's it. Get going. *Do It Now!*

# CHAPTER 4
# Do It Routinely

*We are what we repeatedly do. Excellence, therefore, is not an act but a habit.*

—ARISTOTLE

# Chapter 4 Preview

In this chapter, you will learn how to:

- Organize your schedule and work to operate within large blocks of time.
- Batch your work. Schedule time to process mail and memos all at once. Handle telephone calls, e-mail, and so forth the same way.
- Eliminate low-value information and prevent it from coming to you in the first place.
- Stamp out time-consuming and unnecessary interruptions.
- Hold scheduled one-on-one meetings weekly with your direct reports to improve communication and to process work efficiently.

You will increase your efficiency and effectiveness (your productivity) by working smarter on the right things. The simple key to personal productivity is to batch many job-related activities and do them routinely. The idea is to spend a minimum amount of time on the relatively unimportant things so that you can spend a maximum amount of time on important things.

You must determine the important things—what you should be working on first—and then discover ways to do the work you identify as important more efficiently and effectively.

First, you should assess how you currently spend your time. Next, ask yourself, "Would the results be better if I spent my time working on some other activity?" Then ask yourself, "How could I do the high-level activities more frequently and efficiently?"

*We all need an occasional whack on the side of the head to shake us out of routine patterns, to force us to rethink our problems, and to stimulate us to ask new questions that may lead to other right answers.*
—**ROGER VON OECH,** *A Whack on the Side of the Head: How You Can Be More Creative* **(Warner Books, 1998)**

## KEEP A TIME LOG

To identify precisely how you spend your time, keep a time log. In his landmark book *The Effective Executive* (Harper & Row, 1966), Peter Drucker says that we can't hope to control our time until we know where our time goes. No doubt we think we know where our time goes, but most of us don't. Drucker (p. 27) writes:

> *I sometimes ask executives who pride themselves on their memory to put down their guess as to how they spend their own time. Then I lock these guesses away for a few weeks or months. In the meantime, the executives run an actual time record on themselves. There is never much resemblance between the way these men thought they used their time and their actual records.*

Only by keeping a time log will you get an accurate idea of where your time is being spent. I have often used this technique with clients who are especially busy. Their workload is so great that they do not have a clear picture of the nature of their workload to be able to address it effectively. Keeping a record not only tells them what they spend their time on, it also gives insight into who might be dropping the ball in their area, what functions might not be covered, and how they might be wasting the time of others.

To avoid making this time log an administrative burden, you can simply keep a piece of paper on your desk. As you deal with things, you note what it was, how long it took, and who was involved. Figure 4.1 is a sample form of a time log. Soon categories of things begin to become visible.

After a couple of weeks of keeping records, tally it all up. You will have a pretty good idea where your time goes. You can then start addressing the areas of waste and inefficiency.

## ELECTRONIC TIME LOG

The computer and modern software make it possible to improve time log accuracy and ease the tabulation and evaluation of results. Not only can you keep better track of your own time, you can do so on a department- or company-wide basis. One such software application is Time Tiger (www.timetiger.com).

The software is useful not only as a diagnostic tool. For example, accountants or lawyers who track time for billing purposes, Time Tiger makes the whole process easier and more accurate.

As a planning tool (see Chapter 5, section on "Project Implementation Planning") the software integrates well with project implementation software like Microsoft Project, allowing for accurate planning of time against tasks.

Once again, the principle is that if you wish to gain control over time you must account for it.

## OVERCOME INFORMATION OVERLOAD

We all experience a flood of information. It can be overwhelming and it can blind us to what we should be focused on. Technology has significantly increased the number of ways information and work come our way. There was a time when you only had to cope with the telephone ringing in the office and a mail delivery once a day. Now you have e-mail, faxes, BlackBerrys, PDAs, cell phones, Instant Messaging,

| | Activity | Person | Subject |
|---|---|---|---|
| **7:00** | | | |
| :15 | | | |
| :30 | | | |
| :45 | | | |
| **8:00** | | | |
| :15 | | | |
| :30 | | | |
| :45 | | | |
| **9:00** | | | |
| :15 | | | |
| :30 | | | |
| :45 | | | |
| **10:00** | | | |
| :15 | | | |
| :30 | | | |
| :45 | | | |
| **11:00** | | | |
| :15 | | | |
| :30 | | | |
| :45 | | | |
| **12:00** | | | |
| :15 | | | |
| :30 | | | |
| :45 | | | |
| **1:00** | | | |
| :15 | | | |
| :30 | | | |
| :45 | | | |
| **2:00** | | | |
| :15 | | | |
| :30 | | | |
| :45 | | | |
| **3:00** | | | |
| :15 | | | |
| :30 | | | |
| :45 | | | |
| **4:00** | | | |
| :15 | | | |
| :30 | | | |
| :45 | | | |
| **5:00** | | | |
| :15 | | | |
| :30 | | | |
| :45 | | | |
| **6:00** | | | |
| :15 | | | |
| :30 | | | |
| :45 | | | |

**Figure 4.1** Sample time log form.

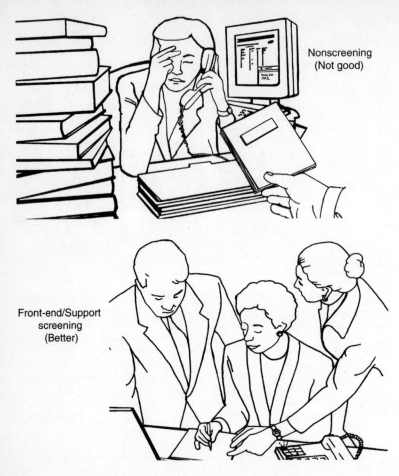

Nonscreening
(Not good)

Front-end/Support
screening
(Better)

**Figure 4.2** Three ways to screen information.

pagers, and a continuous stream of mail from many postal and delivery services. In this information age, we need to know what information we *don't* need as much as we need to know what information we do need.

The best way to overcome information overload is to stop low-value information and tasks from entering your system. Figure 4.2 shows the different ways to screen information. Nonscreening, meaning allowing all information to arrive unfiltered and sorting through it after the fact, is the least effective way of controlling the flow of information to you. A better method of information control would be to have the information screened before it gets to you. Having this done by support staff is better yet. The ideal solution is to carefully analyze all sources of information and eliminate, at the source, the nonessential

Source
screening
(Best)

**Figure 4.2** (*Continued*)

information by removing yourself from the distribution list, canceling the subscription, and so forth.

My friend Ira Chaleff describes it this way. You are sitting by a lake on a summer evening, enjoying the sunset, when you hear bzzzz!!—insects. How do you deal with them? You can wait until they land on you and slap them then, but after a few times it begins to hurt. The same principle applies to the information you receive, whether it's e-mail or interruptions—do you let them all land on you before swatting them? What are some options for your lake house? With screens—whether physical, electronic, or chemical—you keep as many of the things you don't want from landing on you as you can.

Our clients tell us they are more interested in finding ways to cut down the amount of e-mail they get than in ways to process e-mail more efficiently. Processing 250 e-mails a day, no matter how efficiently, still consumes too much time! Screening becomes that much more critical.

The obvious first answer is to critically review the e-mail you get and, if possible, go back to the source of the unnecessary e-mails and ask them to not send it anymore! This may or may not be workable.

But, you can also use technology. All e-mail programs are capable of filtering the e-mail you receive. Many of us know this and activate it for spam and other obvious e-mails we wish to filter. By giving some creative thought to the matter, you can come up with other ways to prevent an overflow of e-mail.

One pharmaceutical company executive was receiving several daily medical bulletins in her inbox, and only occasionally would she have time to read them. She set up a "rule" to have the daily bulletins go into a separate "medical bulletin" folder, and then scheduled a weekly recurring event on her calendar to review all the bulletins at once.

Too often, people abuse the cc option of an e-mail. For different reasons (cultural sensitivity being one), it can be hard to break the habit. One solution could be to establish a rule for having any cc from a certain person about a certain subject go into a folder in the inbox for review, if and when you choose to look at them.

One client had a corporate policy that required storage of all received and sent e-mails for legal purposes. She would spend time daily transferring received and sent mail into a "Legal Hold" folder. She set up a rule so that a copy of all sent and received e-mail automatically went into the Legal Hold folder so she wouldn't have to manually move them each time.

You may have a project due some months in advance. The project may begin with a survey. Send out the survey and establish a rule to have all responses go into a separate folder, bypassing the inbox. When you are ready to tabulate the survey results, go to the folder to find the results.

Analyze your typical e-mail. Is it critical? Can you stop unnecessary e-mail at the source? Can you route it to another person or place? What you do not get in your inbox you don't need to read or handle. (See Chapter 6 for more on this topic.)


## BEYOND THE IN BASKET

Paper in your in basket, voice mail and e-mail messages, telephone calls, and people all clamor for your attention. Add to this all the meetings you must attend, and it's no wonder you feel you rarely accomplish anything important.

I've watched people whose idea of a productive day at work is to spend the entire day at their desks going through the items that come into their in baskets. They are fully occupied doing just those things.

Too much of what comes into your in basket daily is the after-the-fact proof of someone else's accomplishment. It's done, over with, and probably 50% of it is for your information and files. Rarely, if ever, does it make the company money. So often what you process is relatively unimportant. That's why I recommend that you dedicate minimum time to it and get on with your real work.

The way to control this often overwhelming flow of information is to categorize and group it and organize an efficient response to it.

## BATCH THE ROUTINE WORK

The categorizing and grouping of your work might be called "batching." Each piece of paper, each e-mail message, every telephone call, every interruption, and every item you send out is a form of communication. Process similar communications and tasks in batches, reducing waste and motion. You'll complete each task more efficiently.

Many elements of your work can be reduced to simple routines that will let you complete similar tasks in the shortest possible time. These tasks readily lend themselves to batching. The advantages of approaching your work in this way are numerous.

- It is more efficient to process your e-mail two or three times a day on a scheduled basis. You avoid being distracted by things you're not going to act on anyway, and you learn to set time limits and meet those time limits.
- Set aside a time each day to check voice mail and return all phone calls at the same time. Again, this avoids unnecessary interruptions and encourages you to be more effective and efficient in responding to your phone messages.
- Set aside a time in your day for reading. It may be necessary or valuable for you to keep up to date with periodicals and other important reading information. This tends to be assigned lower priority in the face of more urgent demands. But if you set aside a time, for instance, lunchtime, and bring your reading with you,

you'll be able to keep up with your reading responsibilities more effectively.

- It is easier to take a batch of completed work from your out basket and distribute it all at the same time than to get up from your desk each time one piece of work is completed.
- There is less effort involved in doing all filing at once than filing each paper individually.
- You will find batching similar work allows you to prepare and organize yourself for the work one time instead of many times if the work is done randomly.

*What may be done at any time will be done at no time.*
—Scottish Proverb

## SCHEDULE AND AVOID HAVING TO DECIDE

It's important to differentiate between acting on everything as it comes up and always putting things off to do later. There is a way to deal with this. I refer to it as *Do It Now, Later*. Schedule times to do certain work (such as opening and reading your mail, processing your e-mail, returning telephone calls, etc.) and when the time arrives, *Do It Now!* Don't look at it until you are prepared to act. When you do look at it, act on it. *Do It Now, Later*.

If you want to get something done, schedule it. Since these in-box tasks rarely represent the most important part of your job, they are seldom considered priority, so they don't get done. Have you ever noticed when you have made a to-do list of open items, the tasks on the bottom of the list never seem to get done? Urgent tasks always seem to delay action on the merely important ones, and both urgent and important tasks will certainly interfere with paperwork and e-mail. If you constantly prioritize you will never get to these often less critical paperwork and e-mail tasks. But if you do not handle your paperwork and e-mail, they will overwhelm you.

The hidden consequence of this clutter and information overload is to slow down the whole process of your important work. If you have to choose between calling the customer and sorting through your in basket, what are you going to do? If you're like most people, you'll choose the customer, right? But the other things don't get done! What you want to do is avoid putting yourself in the position of constantly having to decide between things. It makes your life harder than it has to be. Instead, schedule a time to go through your in basket and do other routine tasks that can be batched. When the time arrives to do that particular task, do it during the time allotted and move on to the work that is important.

Do you brush your teeth in the morning? "Yes," you say. Do you think about brushing your teeth? Do you prioritize it? Do you wonder, "Am I going to brush my teeth now, or am I going to have a cup of coffee?" Probably not. It's part of a nonthinking routine you've established as part of your habits. You don't burden yourself with lots of thought about it. In fact you hardly give it *any* thought. Through force of habit, you eliminated the steps of conscious decision making. You simply do it routinely. And that's the way you want to handle these simple batched tasks.

## PARKINSON'S LAW AND THE ALLOCATION OF TIME

Parkinson's law says *work tends to fill up (adjust to) the time available or allotted for it*. If you allocate only one hour to complete a certain task you have a much greater chance of finishing the work in that time. If you set a deadline to complete a project by a certain date you will likely figure out how to do it within the time you set for that deadline.

You see this phenomenon with those who tend to work late, beyond the scheduled end of the day. It is common to find people leaving the office at 6:00 PM to be home with their family, and then turning on the computer at 10:00 PM to read their e-mail. When delivering PEP, my first suggestion to participants is that they end the day at the scheduled time and *not* take work home or read e-mail at home. Why? We need a life beyond work. Life already has an established deadline! There are only 24 hours in a day. We are more productive if we have enough sleep, exercise, and cultivate other interests. I think we all know this. More importantly, if you do not establish an "end to the work day," you will not be forced to figure out how to get your work done in the allotted time! So, make this a rule for yourself. Of course there will always be exceptions. You should not live by the exceptions, but instead live by the rule! What are your most important tasks at work? What can you cut out of your day? Get the work done you need to get done, as effectively and as efficiently as you can, in the time you set.

## BLOCKS OF TIME

Working in blocks of time is more efficient and effective than working piecemeal. This applies not only to the batching of similar tasks such as telephone calls or to the handling of incoming mail, but also to project work, sales calls, or a marketing campaign. Peter Drucker suggests that the ideal span of time to work is 90 minutes. You will get more done in a concentrated period of 90 minutes than twice the time in an environment of regular interruptions. Blocking out undisturbed time will greatly increase your productivity. If you manage to get the many little tasks out of the way first, you will be better able to focus during your uninterrupted blocks of time. You'll feel good knowing you've covered all the important issues and organized your time and your work to permit you to do the important things. Giving your mind enough time to get into the heart of the issue is far more productive than being constantly distracted from the work at hand by other tasks that crop up, demanding your attention.

Some of us may not have an office door to close, and so we have to be more creative if we are to enjoy blocks of undisturbed time. One client's company was composed of account officers who worked together in a noisy, open-office environment where the phones rang continuously as clients initiated transactions. In part of the building were several small interview offices. When an account officer needed a block of time to put together a proposal, another officer would cover as he or she used the interview room to peacefully complete the proposal.

Another client would work out of a home office one day per week. This particular client found that working at home afforded him the time he needed for strategic planning and prospecting for new business.

## BATCHING TELEPHONE CALLS

Cell phones have made it much easier for us to keep in touch. That may be exactly what is wrong with them! In the not so distant past you could at least avoid the phone on the way home or after hours. This is not the case today. How can you make this tool work for you rather than you working for it?

If the nature of your job permits, decide that you will not accept calls haphazardly throughout the work day; instead, you will return calls perhaps three or four times during the day. Accept calls a select number of times a day—from 9:00 AM to 9:30 AM, 11:30 AM to noon, and

4:00 PM to 5:00 PM. If you have an administrative assistant have him or her filter your calls and take complete messages at other times. This doesn't mean you want your assistant to hold your calls—it means that you establish a routine: You take phone calls at certain times, except in specific cases. Of course, you then have to define those specific cases. You will probably accept calls from an important client or your immediate supervisor, for example, and you will want to establish clear parameters for emergency calls.

Be sure each office staff member clearly understands the new procedure, who and what the exceptions would be, and how messages for you are to be taken. To return a call you have to understand the message.

"Bill called" is not acceptable by itself. Ask assistants to take *complete, correct* messages. Train your assistants in how to find out what Bill wants and when Bill will be available to discuss the subject: "Bill called to schedule an appointment with the sales team in New York. He will be available all afternoon at such-and-such number." This allows you to prepare yourself for the call. You know what the call is all about, and you know when you can reach him. When you reach Bill, you can have your calendar open and suggest several times and alternative days when you're available to meet. You'll impress Bill and wrap up the call in minimal time.

If you do not have an assistant to screen your calls, use voice mail or an answering service. Create a voice mail message that conveys the same information:

*"Hello, this is Frank. I'm not available to take your call at the moment. If you would leave a complete message, I will prepare for our conversation and get back to you as soon as I can. I normally return phone calls between 11:30 AM and noon, eastern time. Please let me know if that's a convenient time for you. If it isn't, please suggest another time you might be available."*

Now, you have to stick to the new procedure. Stick to the routine of returning all phone calls at a given time in the day, and stick to your procedure of refusing calls at any other time (within the guidelines you establish).

In this way, you'll be prepared to return your calls, and you can organize yourself for them. You can consult files or documents before returning a call. You can have all pertinent material in front of you so you don't waste time. Treat your calls precisely as you treat the items in your in basket—one at a time, working through them to completion. In scheduling these call times allow sufficient flexibility to handle calls that depend on varying time zones, emergencies, and other special circumstances.

## One More Thing!

I highly recommend that you turn off your cell phone after 5 PM when you leave from work and don't turn it back on until you arrive at work the following morning. I realize that some of you will object strongly to being out of touch. I understand that in some industries, this would be impossible. A doctor must be on call. A real estate agent must be on call. But the vast majority of us have jobs that are supposed to end at a specific time of day. Keeping your cell phone on allows people to be in touch with you at times when you should be taking care of your own private life. You may be surprised to learn if you do turn off your cell phone at the end of your scheduled workday, you will begin to figure out how to get the work done within the hours you've allocated for it. Those who would likely want to get in touch with you will also discover that they have to be a bit brighter and sharper about getting in touch during the working hours. The best way to control a cell phone is to turn it off.

## BATCHING E-MAIL

It is vital to apply the *Do It Now* principle when processing e-mail (as well as paper mail, faxes, and voice mail messages). Many of the problems you experience coping with the volumes of correspondence you receive will be resolved by simply doing it now. But *when* to *Do It Now* is important.

Some e-mail applications have a built-in beeper or flashing visual signal alert function, so every time you receive a new message the computer alerts you. The alert prompts you to look at the incoming message, and because you are in the middle of something else or not prepared to spend the time to answer the message your tendency is to do it later. This is not the way to process your e-mail. I suggest you turn off the alert function and instead set up times in your schedule to process your e-mail. Processing e-mail needs to be done more than once a day. E-mail has, to some degree, become a substitute for the telephone and face-to-face meetings and needs to be acted upon promptly, although, in most environments, it should not command the same immediacy as the telephone.

How do you handle this? I suggest you handle your e-mail three or four times a day. Seldom do people expect a response to an e-mail immediately. If you process your e-mail regularly, say first thing in the morning, before lunch, and before leaving for the day, this is normally quite sufficient. Schedule times in your calendar to process the e-mail. Establish time parameters and work to get the e-mail done in those times, if at all possible. If you cannot, then look for ways to cut down on the messages. (More on this later.)

Remember, when I say *process* I do not mean look at and decide to respond later. I mean complete it now. If it is not possible to complete it, take it as far as you possibly can and write a reminder to follow-through on whatever actions may still be needed. If the e-mail represents a large block of work time, schedule it into your calendar and file the message away.

When processing e-mail, follow the four Ds as described below:

1. *Do it now.* Read, respond, and act on the e-mail to completion.
2. *Delegate it.* If it's something someone else can or should do, pass it on to them now.
3. *Designate it.* Create a task if it's something that's going to take you some time to do. Use a calendar to schedule the task.
4. *Discard (or file) it.*

By following the four Ds, you will have processed each e-mail and at the end have an empty inbox.

---

*Tip:* Our IBT Canadian office advises that people do not start the day by opening their e-mail. Instead start the day doing the most important task. Once done (or progressed as desired) then open your e-mail inbox. E-mail can be a distraction from the most vital tasks. So do them first!

---

## PAPER MAIL/MEMOS

Deal with your mail and internal office memos once a day at a set time, perhaps first thing in the morning before the normal meetings and activities begin. Depending on the nature of your work, allow 30 to 60 minutes to process all of the paper that accumulates in your in basket during the day. If you have an administrative assistant, have him or her hold all incoming paperwork arriving after you complete your pass at the in basket. Ask your assistant to sort the incoming material into logical categories and to use a divider system to organize incoming material and make it easy for you to process. After purging the inevitable junk mail, have your assistant put the incoming papers into your in basket at the end of the day and place items for other people to deal with in their baskets. Then you don't have to go through other people's materials. Included in your incoming papers would be any papers from your tickler file that are scheduled for your attention the next day.

Some managers invite their administrative assistants to sit in with them while they deal with their in basket. In this case, the assistant files as they go along, notes instructions, and generally helps the manager process the work quickly. This, by the way, is how I advise managers to train new administrative assistants. The manager should process the paperwork out loud, so the assistant gets a sense for how the manager deals with things, what is important to the manager, and what the manager wants to see and not see. I find a couple of weeks of this equals a year's worth of experience working together.

Whether you work with an assistant or not, don't just sort through your papers. *Do* each item, one by one, responding, routing, reading, and filing as you go along. If a paper is part of a working project you will be acting on at a scheduled time in the future, file it immediately in your working file. If a paper prompts an origination from you, originate it now. If it's something you need to discuss with a subordinate or your boss and it's not a burning issue, file it in your working file under his or her name for discussion at your scheduled meeting time. If it's something to read, read it. If the paper represents a task to be done in the future, write it down in your task list. Note the specific next step.

Make no exceptions to the rule. This is a moment of truth. If a paper represents two or three hours' work, schedule a time to deal with it, and file the paper into its appropriate working file or the scheduled date in your tickler file. Note the task in your task list. But mainly *Do It Now* and empty your inbox of all papers that were there. Some won't be all that important, but deal with them, anyway.

Some might say looking at your papers once a day is not enough. Well, I disagree. Very important issues normally find their way to you in the form of telephone calls, personal visits, or e-mail. Since most people do not deal with their paper promptly, they don't depend on it for hot issues that need to be dealt with in a matter of minutes. If you *did* process your paper completely every day you would surprise your coworkers with your promptness!

## READING

Your reading should be handled in the same way. Set aside a block of time and do it however works best for you. Some of your reading will be done when you process your e-mail, mail, and memos. Remember when you pick up a piece of paper you are going to deal with it then and there. Some people do their reading during the morning commute by bus or train; some do it during plane flights; others take a few minutes at the end of the workday to do their reading and organize for the coming workday. I do my reading during my lunch break. The important thing is to find a time to do it and establish this as a routine. Assign yourself a time, schedule it, and do it.

*When* you read is one issue; *how* you read is another. Speed reading can cut your reading time in half by training you to look at the material from a concept, sentence, paragraph, or page perspective, instead of word by word, which is how most of us have been taught to read. There is no loss of content comprehension. You simply comprehend more, faster!

## WEEKLY ONE-ON-ONE MEETINGS

Weekly one-on-one meetings between the boss and his or her direct reports come under the heading of routine.

*One-on-one meetings make for efficient contact time between busy coworkers who have to maintain close contacts in their work.*

If the only way colleagues can see you is by sticking their heads in during the day at random, you will be constantly interrupted. They will feel guilty about disturbing you, but they know they must if they are going to get the job done. You won't be prepared for discussion on the subject they disturb you about. Or vice versa if you are the one interrupting.

You may argue that you can't handle another meeting. However, many managers are managers in name only. With downsizing, companies are forcing managers to have many more duties than simply managing. You need an efficient way to keep in touch with those who answer to you and who get the work done.

This is not a team or group meeting. It's one-on-one. Maintain a file for every person you meet with one-on-one, and during the course of the week, collect any nonpriority items you need to discuss. Also, each person who reports to you should maintain a similar folder, covering items they need to talk about with you.

Schedule one-on-one meetings for the same time every week. If it isn't scheduled, people can't depend on it, and they will revert to coming to see you at any odd time. If you travel often or a holiday period makes it difficult to keep to the same schedule, make it a point at the end of your one-on-one to schedule the next one-on-one meeting, taking the holiday into account.

Remember, these meetings cover nonpriority items that crop up and can wait a few days to be resolved or answered, not things that demand an immediate solution.


## DAILY MEETING WITH ADMINISTRATIVE ASSISTANT

Years ago, a senior executive secretary for a *Fortune* 500 company taught me the value of a 15-minute one-on-one meeting with the company president at the start of each day. She was the epitome of competence. To call her a secretary doesn't do her justice. She was a key operations person who made her boss successful. She was not only the president's gatekeeper, she was his right hand. If he needed something done, he would give it to her.

According to her, the most important time of the day was the 15 minutes they spent first thing in the morning. It was her time to have his undivided attention, pass on important information, go over the day's schedule, and most important, get a sense of the issues and priorities he was working on. Armed with this information, she was able to make sure the day was focused on what he needed to accomplish. If a person or call came in that forwarded his priorities, she knew he would want to know immediately. It made the support she provided that much more relevant.

For high-level executives time is precious. The administrative assistant (AA) is the exec's most critical resource for managing that time. A brief meeting at the beginning of the day will ensure the exec utilizes the AA to the maximum. Yes, the AA is likely in and out all day. That is not enough. Try the one-on-one meeting as described earlier. You will be surprised at the result.

*Time is the coin of your life. It is the only coin you have, and only you can determine how it will be spent. Be careful lest you let others spend it for you.*

—CARL SANDBURG

## DEALING WITH INTERRUPTIONS

Not all interruptions are bad, of course. There are actually some good interruptions. If your associate pokes his head in your doorway and says, "Hey, listen, I had this bright idea about how to get a sale, and I'd like to make a call," that's what I'd call a good interruption.

Still, there are more ways to cut down on unwanted interruptions. Here are some tried-and-true ways that should sound familiar to you:

### Do It Now!
- Clean up backlogs so you're not dealing with their consequences.
- Handle things by their due dates to reduce requests for status reports.

### Do It "Right" Now
- Handle things completely and correctly to reduce (re-do) requests.
- Give clear and complete instructions to subordinates to reduce their requests for clarification and your own frustrations when things are not done correctly the first time.
- Remember that it is your job to educate your employees in how to complete both routine tasks and larger jobs.

### Communicate It "Right" Now
- Give full information when leaving messages to reduce telephone tag.
- Require complete messages be taken when others call you.
- Use communication methods that permit full messages and do not interrupt current work, such as e-mail and voice mail.

### "Take a Stand" Now

- Deal with interruptions by stating your time constraints: "Jim, I have 20 minutes to complete this report for a meeting. Let me stop by your office after that meeting and we'll discuss this. Is 2:30 all right with you?"
- Reinforce this by standing up to deal with walk-in interruptions.
- Lend support to creating a culture with fewer interruptions.
- Begin batching your communications.

By batching work you can cut down on interruptions (see Figure 4.3), allowing you to focus better on the work on hand.

## RESPECT OTHER PEOPLE'S TIME

Some people are so determined to finish what is in their hand, they get into the habit of going to others' offices and interrupting them. They want to complete what they are doing. They give no consideration to their coworkers. This can be especially irritating when coming from the "boss." In their arrogance, they consider anything they are doing must be more important than what a subordinate is doing. What makes this particularly irksome is that the behavior is not selective. It is habitual. Of course there will be occasions in which interrupting someone to deal with something important is justified. But too often, I run into someone (boss or otherwise) who constantly does this. Remember, this habit is most likely inefficient for you, too! If you are inclined to do this, stop it. Respect others' time. Use another channel to get your task progressed or done. It will make for a more productive and happier environment.

## MAKING IT WORK

You may think: "Hey, I don't want to schedule my life down to the minute," or "This represents an ideal world, and my office is far from ideal." These scheduled activities should require no more than 20% of your day. Since all my research shows that you are spending well over *half* of your day on these things now, you can thank me for giving you back at least 25% of your day.

I don't like having my day scheduled to the minute, either. But most of what I'm asking you to do here is to handle the mindless and boring tasks efficiently and routinely. We have to do the mundane if we're to

**Failure to Batch Communications**

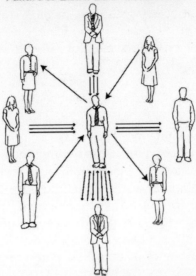

**Multiple Interruptions Caused and Received**

**Batched Communications**

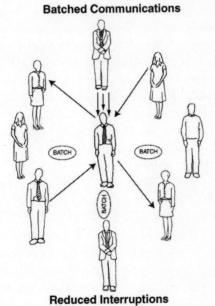

**Reduced Interruptions**

**Figure 4.3**  Batching communications reduces interruptions.

concentrate on what we are truly being paid for. So, why not just face up to it and do it? Get it over with in as painless a fashion as possible. Then the remainder of your day can be made up of blocks of time to concentrate and focus on the meaningful activities of your work.

## PITFALLS

One problem people sometimes face early on in learning to work this way is that they sometimes choose the wrong time to do certain things. You may decide to return all your phone calls at 4:00 PM every day, regardless of circumstances, when in fact, because you're on the West Coast, it's impossible for you to reach anyone east of Denver at that time. The logical thing to do is to allow a few moments between 8:00 AM and 9:00 AM for any calls you have to place to the East Coast; there's no reason you can't take care of this business before moving on to your in basket, for example.

Or you may decide to answer your mail and memos once a day at 10:00 AM without fail. Of course, that's exactly the time the new staff meeting is scheduled or, for reasons known only to them, the Postal Service readjusts its schedule and your daily mail is delivered at 3:00 PM. For whatever reason, after just one day it's quite possible for your new schedule to fail. And since it fails, you assume it has failed completely, and you give up the effort, instead of examining what happened and trying to reschedule your planned activities to fit reality. You may discover it's more feasible to draft memos between 11:45 AM and 12:15 PM, or even noon to 12:30 PM since you seldom get out the door to lunch until then anyway, and schedule 3:30 PM to 4:00 PM to respond to the day's mail. The point is, you may have to try several times before you find the schedule that works best for you.

Trial and error is often required in getting the job done and in learning new ways to get jobs done. For example, you may have to have people cover for you while you do some of the batched work we talked about. If you have a customer service job, for example, you may not be able to turn off your phone. Or your work may depend on walk-in customers, and you may never know when a customer is going to arrive. Certainly, when customers do walk in, you want to see them and answer their needs.

I had a client who had five employees to deal with 3,000 customers, mostly by telephone and e-mail. But every day they could expect 10 or so unannounced customers to arrive to see their account representatives. The visits were mainly social and considered more or less a waste of time. The employees wanted to treat the customers well. They wanted to give good service, but the unannounced arrivals created havoc with their schedules and work. This problem existed for years and nothing seemed to make it go away until the department was reorganized so each account rep was on duty to see all unannounced customers one day per week, leaving four days per week when each rep was able to get on with his or her work. I can't tell you how many other solutions were tried, though, before they used this rather simple one and found that it worked.

As you attempt to put some of these principles into practice, you'll find some trial and error is required, too. Persistence counts. If you work on the problem, you'll come up with not only a solution, but a solution that works for you.

We all know how difficult it is to overcome habits and years of conditioning. Habitual behaviors usually don't change on the first attempt. Your first 14 tries may appear to be failures. But then something clicks on the 15th try, and you find everything falling into place. Even when you do finally get into the new habit, it isn't necessarily easier to do unpleasant or boring tasks. Every time I wake at 5:00 AM to go running, I find it is tough. But, scheduling the routine behavior helps me to do it. If the running were not a habit, I would surely find it even tougher, and I would likely not do it at all.

Let scheduling and simple habits make life easier for you.

## FOLLOW-UP FOR CHAPTER 4

**1.** Work smarter. You can increase your efficiency and effectiveness (productivity) by working smarter. Only you can determine what requires and deserves your attention. Regardless of what those things are, you can make more time for them by working smarter on everything. Simple routines to handle the mundane tasks can help you do exactly that.

**2.** Analyze your time. If you've never analyzed how and where you spend your time, this can be very useful. Use a time log to keep track of what you do and how long it takes. You'll be amazed at how much time you spend on certain items and how little time you spend on others. Once you know what you're doing, you can work on how you do it.

**3.** Don't allow low-value tasks or low-value information to enter your system. Both clog your ability to produce. Screen them out entirely. Delegate tasks appropriately. Direct information you don't use to someone else's attention. Dedicate minimal time to routine work, such as the incoming mail. Take care of it promptly and routinely, and move on to high-value work.

**4.** Learn how to batch work. Return phone calls a select number of times daily, rather than allowing them to constantly interrupt your work. Do the same with your incoming mail. Set aside a time each day to work through each item to completion, or schedule items to work on at appropriate times in the short-term future. If you batch work instead of letting unimportant tasks dominate your day, you'll find you have about 25% more time to dedicate to important work. Answering phone messages, responding to memos, and handling your e-mail are all tasks you should handle by batching.

**5.** *Do It Now, Later* means sticking to a schedule. If you're in the middle of a report when your mail is delivered, continue to work on the report. Schedule 30 minutes daily to handle your mail and do it then. Don't break off in the middle of one task to take on another. If you do, both are likely to end up unfinished as the second task is interrupted by a third task.

**6.** Schedule tasks (and you have less to worry about). If scheduled, you simply do them and move on. If you allot an hour for a particular task, you will likely complete it within an hour. If you allot a day for the same task, you will likely take all day to complete it.

**7.** Schedule weekly one-on-one meetings for routine items concerning your direct reports. This will eliminate most interruptions and will allow you regular time periods to touch base with one another regarding ongoing projects and personal items. You should maintain a file for each of your people and make a habit of dropping reminders into it to prompt your meeting agendas. Your direct reports should keep a similar file for you, to prompt their discussion during these meetings. Remember, these meetings are for nonpriority items that can wait up to a week to be resolved, and not for emergencies.

**8.** Review the steps you can use to eliminate interruptions and then put them into practice.

# CHAPTER 5
# Plan It Now!

*There is a law in psychology that if you form a picture in your mind of what you would like to be, and you keep and hold that picture there long enough, you will soon become exactly as you have been thinking.*

—WILLIAM JAMES

*The important thing is to start—to create a plan and then follow it step by step no matter how small or large each one by itself might seem.*

—CHARLES LINDBERGH

# Chapter 5 Preview

In this chapter, you will learn:

- That time flies by when you are in a state of preoccupation. Thinking about what you are supposed to do instead of planning efficiently is a major cause of wasted time.
- That action follows clarity of picture. If you have a clear picture of what you are to do, you will act on it. If the picture is fuzzy, you will hesitate. Planning gives clarity of picture.
- How to establish what is important to you.
- How to write down your goals (those that will define what you value).
- How to establish an efficient planning process by setting aside time each week to organize yourself, review your goals and plans, and plan out the new week.

This may surprise you, but the motto for the planning step of the Personal Efficiency Program (PEP) is *Plan It Now!*

One purpose of planning is to get *clarity,* to know what you ought to be doing on a day-to-day basis as well as on a long-term basis. Too many people do very little planning, particularly when their own work is involved. One reason why the personal calendar, planner, or organizer (Day-Timer, Franklin/Covey Planner, etc.) has been so popular is that people see it as a tool to help them get organized, to plan things in advance, and to keep track of work done.

Some mistakenly consider the mental activities they engage in when they're driving to work or when they're taking a shower to be "planning" for work. Although you may be thinking about work, I would hardly call it planning. Instead, it's an inefficient form of thinking that provides little or no real clarity.

Some people feel that any and all planning is a waste of time. They say the time spent in planning doesn't produce that many benefits. If you plan inefficiently, that can be true. If what you plan is not what you do, it is wasteful. A set plan is good only if it is being implemented and accomplished. If what you do is what you plan, then planning is meaningful.

If you feel that you're under stress at work; that you have too much to do, and too little time to do it; that you're out of control; or that you're simply not accomplishing the things most important to you, the cause is often poor planning or the lack of planning. In that case, you'll find that the products you produce bear a resemblance to the bumper sticker "Plan Ahead," where the word "Ahead" is all crunched up on the right side.

That's typical, primarily because people don't connect planning to what they do personally. They think of planning in terms of the huge project their department is undertaking during this fiscal quarter—a project so huge that they'll all get together for a meeting and figure out what to do. But when it comes to their daily work, they don't attach proper importance to planning.

## PURPOSE OF PLANNING

The purpose of the planning process is to get a clear idea—a clear mental picture—of what you need to do. A planning process can be considered effective only if it provides you with a clear picture, because you can't act without a picture. In his book *The Management of Time* (Prentice-Hall, 1959), James T. McCay writes:

> *The pictures in your mind control your actions. If you have no picture; if you can't make out what is going on, you don't act. If your pictures are cloudy and confused, you act hesitantly. If your pictures are clear and accurate, you act definitely and effectively.*

Planning enables you to get these clear pictures. Planning that fails to provide such images falls short of the mark and isn't true planning.

When doing PEP with a large group, we start out with an orientation, usually in a conference room with everyone seated around a table. I often ask: "How many people in here do a daily action plan?" Perhaps half the people raise their hands. The rest don't even commit themselves to daily action plans. Too often these daily to-do lists have failed for them in the past, and they're reluctant to try them again.

Have you ever started the day with a list of things to do and come to the end of the day with none of the tasks done? If so, you know how many of these people feel. Daily action plans can weigh one down: They're the evidence of unfinished business. There are several reasons for unfinished lists: You might have tried to do too much. You may not have considered the unexpected and the time that would be consumed. The daily list may have been far too general. Proper planning successfully deals with these and many other issues that can make a daily plan a disappointment rather than a useful work tool. What is proper planning?

To give an example, let's look at what it takes to make a movie. Three distinct steps are involved in the production of a movie: preproduction, production, and postproduction. Of the three, the most time-consuming element of making the movie is preproduction. The script is only the starting point. The most essential planning document in the preproduction phase is known as the storyboard, a detailed, artistic representation of every single scene that will make up the movie.

Picture a sheet of paper filled only with empty boxes; sometimes, you'll even find them in the familiar shape of a television screen. These boxes make up the frames for each scene. Artists sketch in rough outlines to represent what is seen at every point of filming: which people are in a particular scene; what they say; whether a scene is shot in close-up or with a long lens; where the lights are; the step-by-step progression from one shot to the next; the combination of shots adding up to a single scene. These are all part of the much larger whole—a motion picture.

Why spend so much time and effort on a storyboard? Because one of the most expensive parts of moviemaking is the on-location shooting. Once production is under way, with 200 cast and crew members standing around, you want to waste little time and effort, not to mention money, telling people where they stand and what they do next. That's what preproduction is for, not production. With millions of dollars invested, you simply don't waste time when adequate planning and preparation will save you that time and effort.

In the motion picture industry, the need for planning is obvious and the technique of planning has been refined to meet that industry's particular needs. Yet in business and industry in general, there is little formal planning, especially the planning of day-to-day activities.

Take a mental step back from your own company, and you'll see that most of the people you work with every day don't have any formal planning in their work. We see people showing up for work without any script or preproduction planning, merely hoping to handle the fallout for eight or more hours. In motion picture terms, they're on the set every day of the workweek, the cameras are rolling, and they don't know what to say, where to stand, or what to do.

## PLANNING PRINCIPLES

Planning has three components: prioritizing tasks, managing time, and being well enough organized to execute the plans easily. By the time you have reached this chapter, you should be well enough organized to execute your plans easily. Let's examine the other components.

### Prioritizing—Task Management

You cannot discuss planning without also discussing priorities. You have, no doubt, detected my wariness about prioritizing. Priorities are too often used as an excuse not to act. And priorities can create a mess when you are faced with urgent versus important matters. Nevertheless, if you neglect priorities, especially with the volume of work expected of us and the extreme time pressure many of us are under, you are likely to fail.

My friend from the Netherlands describes it like this: Planning is the activity of determining your priorities and then managing the time to deal with those priorities. To determine priorities one must have a clear picture of one's goals or objectives and then compare tasks against them. You must determine if the tasks expected of you align with the steps necessary to achieve your goals/objectives. Decide whether you are the one to execute these priority tasks or if they can or should be delegated to another. If you delegate them, then follow through to see that they are completed.

Task management can be an especially useful tool for those who have little discretionary time. Call center or help desk employees and bank tellers are examples of those whose tasks are dictated by those contacting them. The less control you have of your own time the more you need to distinguish between very valuable and less valuable issues.

## Time Management

Time management could be described as the art of making the best use of time. Once you know what you need to do and how best to do it (task management), you need to make the best use of time to get it done. When planning your day, week, month, or year, you consider the tasks to be done and the time elements involved. Proper management of time includes:

- Routines being established and scheduled into different periods of the day (daily batched work like responding to e-mail, weekly routines like batched meetings with direct reports, monthly routine for end-of-month close-out processes, etc.).
- Open- and closed-door policies scheduled into the day. When do you need uninterrupted time to concentrate?
- Considering your biorhythm when scheduling creative work. When in the day are you most energetic (good for work requiring creative juices)? When are you least energetic (good for boring tasks requiring less concentrated thought—filing, for example)?
- Setting aside periods for planning, both short and long term. Daily planning might require a few minutes; weekly and monthly planning might take an hour; and yearly long-term planning may take a few days to complete.
- The type of calendar system you use—paper for your personal use or electronic, which may be accessible and possibly added to by others. The more other people have access to your time

planning, the more you have to schedule time for your own priorities. Does your secretary schedule your meetings? How well does he or she know your preferences for planning meetings, quiet time, routine tasks, and so on? The type of calendar (daily view, weekly view, or monthly view) determines the way you perceive time.

- Lastly, a critical part of time management is protecting your time!

> *If you spend half your time planning, you will get it done twice as fast.*
> — GERMAN PROVERB

### The Time It Takes to Plan: Is It Worth It?

If you increase your planning time, you will be able to reduce time spent in "administrivia" and running around playing "catch up."
Most of us work long hours and work hard. Why do we complain about being lost in "administrivia"? For one thing, no matter how clever we get, we find "administrivia" will take from 10% to 25% of your working time, depending on your job. The average person in industry, before PEP, typically spends less than two hours per week planning his or her own work. If you do the math, that's about 18 minutes a day—the equivalent of the time you spend in the shower! That's fine; don't stop that daily planning exercise (or shower for that matter!). But take it further to reduce time spent in "administrivia" and interruptions. Spend more time planning!

## PEP PLANNING PROCESS

Six general categories of planning are taught in PEP:

1. Daily plan.
2. Weekly plan.
3. Project implementation plan.
4. Strategic plan.
5. Goal setting.
6. Values.

## DAILY PLANNING

I've already mentioned a common complaint about daily plans. Too often, due to the unexpected, the daily plan is only partially done before it turns into a major disappointment. For some people, it seems, daily plans are only a mocking reminder of what didn't get done.

In the meantime, it's vital that you understand the importance of spending some time each day to plan your activities. Some prefer to do this at day's end, before going home; some prefer the morning, before other things get in the way. Whenever you choose to do this planning, you can use your calendar ("diary," as the British say) to write down the day's tasks.

To make daily planning an efficient and quick process, I suggest you create your daily plan from a weekly plan. With the larger document in front of you, you can then divide the week's work into manageable chunks to be accomplished each day, knowing every day that you're working toward a larger goal.

## WEEKLY PLANNING

Once a week you should examine all of your sources of work as shown in Figure 5.1. By "sources of work" I mean all of your working files, including your projects; your calendar for deadlines, scheduled activities, and reminders; your tickler file system for the things that will be showing up during the upcoming week; your pending matters (pending basket and pending files—including electronic files like an e-mail folder for any e-mail awaiting feedback before you can complete it); and any logbook you may use to keep a record of the things you must do.

For example, let's assume you're currently handling eight projects. Perhaps two of these projects are taking up the majority of your time, and the other six are moving along to one degree or another. You have other items in your pending box as well, including plans for a business trip, and your calendar shows six meetings this week with various department heads and customers. Your tickler file contains items you have to check on at various dates to guarantee they'll be finished on time. You're also surrounded by a lot of little pieces of paper with various reminders of tasks that you need to do. (Or better yet, you may have a computer program or logbook you use to consolidate these reminders in one place, instead of having lots of little pieces of paper.) In other words, to keep up with everything you have to do, you really

## WHY WEEKLY PLANNING?

Events change rapidly and it is not feasible for most people to plan a month in advance in detail. On the other hand, if one plans only a day in advance, there is insufficient lead time to get critical things done. For most people, weekly planning is the most effective planning interval.

### CREATING YOUR WEEKLY ACTION PLAN

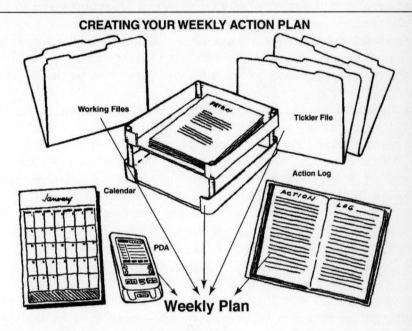

**Figure 5.1**   Create your weekly plan.

have to consult half a dozen sources. I suggest you go through all of these sources once a week. During that time, prioritize these various items and plan out your week.

Take the time to look back through your calendar to determine how much of your time is consumed by unexpected, unplanned-for work. Some of this will be boss-imposed time, when you catch the fallout from some higher-up who seems, without fail, to delegate in your direction at the most inopportune time of the day (or week, or month). Some of this will simply be unforeseen work that requires your attention, eating up time you had intended to devote to other work. Whatever the source, it's inevitable that at least some portion of your day and week—perhaps 25%, perhaps as much as 50%—will be given to this type of work.

Whatever the amount, plan your workweek based on the average amount of time left to you. If half of your time is used unexpectedly, you can reasonably plan for only the other 50% of your time to be filled with genuinely productive work of your own planning. By allowing time for the unexpected—actually the unidentified—you maintain your flexibility, you allow time for the things you know are going to crop up (even if you don't know in advance what they are), and you don't overload yourself to the point that you're actually scheduling your week for work that would really take one and a half weeks. You've *planned for the unplanned,* and you can define the rest of your week with clarity and purpose.

By identifying and prioritizing the actions to be done in the next week, you simplify daily planning. Prioritizing is easier, too. If it's important, it will be on your weekly plan. If it isn't important, it won't be there. You only have to decide your priorities once, during your weekly planning. The advantage to this planning is that you see things in a broader context, so you can make a realistic judgment of how much time you have available to devote to various projects. You don't have to go through the whole decision-making process each time you complete a task, and that in itself takes a lot of the stress out of your work. Choosing what to do any particular day is easier. All you do is look at your calendar and note the reminders you've written down, the meetings that are scheduled, and the work you may have taken on for the coming week. You then take from your weekly plan list those tasks you will do that day. Figure 5.2 shows a sample weekly plan.

## One More Reason to Schedule a WRAP (Weekly Review and Action Plan)

*In the face of sustained attack and unrelenting pressure, fall back—reassess and regroup.*

—SUN TZU, CHINESE MILITARY THEORIST

Most of us are under constant pressure to get things done. Too often there is more to do than can be done in a day or week. It never stops. With a scheduled weekly planning time you have the opportunity to step back, reassess, and regroup.

Setting aside time at the end of the week to do a plan for the new week not only makes for efficient planning time, it also allows you to break from the pressures and get a fresh perspective on your situation.

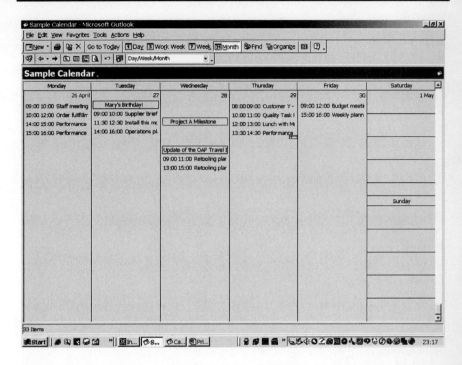

**Figure 5.2** Sample weekly plan in calendar.

We do not typically take the time for a thorough reassessment of our jobs and life, but we should. Your weekly WRAP becomes the time to figure out not only what you should do but also how to do it—the time to think the whole thing through, to see the bigger picture. After all, most tasks are done with some larger end result in mind. With that end result in mind, you can analyze what you need to do (to have, to know) to accomplish the task.

Deciding what should be done first, second, or third takes only a moment. If you schedule tasks across the workweek and do your daily planning based on the larger picture you create, you don't have to spend time thinking about what you need to do day to day or how you're going to do it. You have already done that as part of your weekly plan. Instead, you can focus on the work to be done, and as you complete a task simply get on with doing (not just thinking about) the next one.

Whatever calendar or scheduling tool you prefer, look for one with a week-at-a-glance function. To name just a few of the options available today, you might use a paper calendar system; if you're a corporate user you likely will have either Windows Outlook or Lotus Notes, any

**WEEKLY PLANNING
FORM**

Name: _____

Week Beginning: _____

| Monday | Weekly Plan |
|---|---|
| | (Consult working files, pending tray, calendar, tickler system) |
| | 1. |
| | 2. |
| Tuesday | 3. |
| | 4. |
| | 5. |
| | 6. |
| | 7. |
| Wednesday | 8. |
| | 9. |
| | 10. |
| | 11. |
| | 12. |
| Thursday | 13. |
| | 14. |
| | 15. |
| | **Unplanned Activities Added during Week** |
| Friday | 1. |
| | 2. |
| | 3. |
| Sat/Sun | 4. |
| | 5. |
| | 6. |
| | 7. |

**Figure 5.3**   Sample weekly planning form.

of several types of software for desktop computers, or a handheld electronic organizer. If all the tasks for your weekly plan will actually fit in the weekly calendar view, all the better—there's far less likelihood of important things being overlooked. Figure 5.3 shows a sample weekly planning form.

It is often useful to use your electronic calendar functionality to view your work from a broader time frame than a week. With tools like Microsoft Outlook and Lotus Notes you can very easily move from one view of the future (calendar) to another view, which enables you to make the best possible decisions on your planning process and implementation.

Often decisions regarding even a weekly plan are influenced by the monthly view and perhaps the daily view. Looking at these

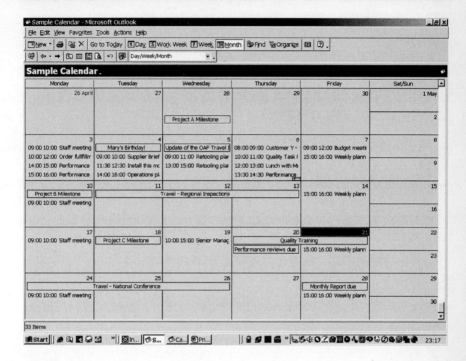

**Figure 5.4** Sample monthly planning.

various views is probably needed to best make planning decisions. The flexibility of viewing, with whatever degree of detail one needs to make the best planning decisions by moving between views, should be reinforced regardless of whether the planning is daily, weekly, or monthly. Figure 5.4 shows a sample monthly planning format.

So, what's the point of this whole weekly planning process? This is the time for you to get an overview of your job. This is the time for you to organize yourself and prepare for the new week. It's a time for you to maintain your organized state. It's a time for you to step back, reassess, and regroup. It's a time for you to take your objectives, goals, and dreams and put them into action steps.

In his book *Project Planning* (Simon & Schuster, 1947), Frank Bettger, one of the most influential salesmen of the twentieth century, called his weekly planning time his "self-organization day." He said:

*It is surprising how much I can get done when I take enough time for planning, and it is perfectly amazing how little I get done without it. I prefer to work on a tight schedule four and a half days a week and get somewhere than be working all the time and never get anywhere. (p. 25)*

## SHAPING THE DIARY—A MONTHLY PLANNING PROCESS FOR SENIOR EXECUTIVES

My friend and partner from the United Kingdom, Jay Hurwitz, has been working with top-level executives of the United Kingdom's largest corporations and has designed a highly successful planning process he calls Shaping the Diary. As part of their planning routines, Jay gets the executives to shape their calendars once a month, usually at midmonth for the subsequent month. Monthly planning is more appropriate for high-level executives as they tend to book important meetings further ahead in the calendar and are involved a bit less in day-to-day operational issues that pop up unexpectedly.

This is what he has each executive do:

1. Take a blank sheet of paper and create the following format:
2. List no more than eight broad actions that account for 100% of your time expenditure. For example:

   - Management team meeting.
   - Managing direct reports.
   - Personnel matters.
   - Budgets.
   - Walkabouts, branch visits, customer visits.
   - In tray.
   - Project work.
   - Other.

3. Once the broad actions are listed, estimate what percentage of your time is currently being spent in each category. Note the percentages in the Now column. Don't worry about your estimates adding up to 100% on the first go. Just take your gut feelings. After you have noted a gut feeling percentage beside each action, adjust them if they do not total 100%.
4. Ask yourself if there is some aspect of your job that you are not doing, that you feel you ought to be doing, and that is not on your list (e.g., think time, review time, or planning time). Add it to the list.

**5.** Consider how you would like to ideally spend your time in the future. For example:

- If there was an item that was added in step 4, start with that. What percentage of your time would you like to spend on that action? Note it under the Future column.
- Consider each of the other actions and your percentages and note those in the Future column.
- Be realistic. If you are currently spending 25% of your time in management team meetings and note 0% for that item in the future, you're not being realistic. Attendance at management team meetings is probably beyond your control.

**6.** Block out chunks of time in your calendar over the next month (or the month after if you are already fully scheduled for the next month) just for those actions showing a larger percentage in the Future column than the Now column. This will likely ensure that you *make* the time for these items and actually bring about the change.

Do not block out chunks of time for all of your actions. This would make the diary too rigid and would not allow for responsiveness to developing events.

> *The secret of getting ahead is getting started. The secret of getting started is breaking your complex and overwhelming tasks into small manageable tasks and then starting on the first one.*
> —MARK TWAIN

## PROJECT IMPLEMENTATION PLANNING

In addition to the weekly planning process we've discussed, we're going to look closely at another type of planning called project planning.

We've already touched on creating your working files and how these files should represent the basic objectives and projects you're working on. Each file may represent hundreds of hours of work over a long period of time and can be pretty overwhelming.

Have you ever heard the question, "How do you eat an elephant?" One fellow told me, "With lots of ketchup!" The answer, though, is one bite at a time, and this is one secret to increased productivity. If you take the time to break down larger, more complex activities into manageable and detailed tasks—as with strategic and tactical planning—you will increase your personal productivity, whether you're discussing long- or short-term goals, or multitask objectives. I cannot stress too strongly the importance of this concept when it comes to productivity and the accomplishment of work and life goals.

> ### *Little by little does the trick.*
> ### —AESOP

Most of us know in general terms what we need to do. In fact, in my experience too much of our time is consumed in considering what we need to do, thinking about how to do it, and becoming preoccupied with the details of the work involved—none of which actually accomplish anything.

*Project planning*, however, is the process of creating storyboards for each of your life and work goals. All of us are familiar with project planning in the broad sense. An example would be the yearly budget for the company or division and the goals set to achieve the budget. The preproduction phase of making a motion picture can be considered a project plan. In fact, the preproduction phase, or the budget process, is made up of many individual project plans. All of the goals and objectives, both professional and personal, we work on daily, and the individual actions to accomplish these goals can be called project plans. My favorite definition (from a colleague in the United Kingdom, Ron Hopkins) of a project is:

> *That series of connected action points, which, when each and all are completed, bring into being a specific, visualized objective or result.*

Each of your objectives and goals should have its own project plan.

The storyboard (project plan) is a set of clear mental pictures of each specific action required to move you step-by-step toward the accomplishment of the goal. Devising the project plan prompts you to explore how best to do it, in what sequence, with what resources, in how much time, with whom, and in concert with what other projects or activities that need to be done.

If complete, your working files will represent each of your work objectives. A project plan should be drawn up and placed in each of your working files. Deadlines for the tasks should be noted, along with the person responsible for the task. The project plan prompts you to do things to accomplish your goals because you've visualized them clearly and analyzed the work required to accomplish them. If the tasks are defined in detail, each one can be done in short time, and accomplishing each task will result in continuous progress toward the larger objective.

When you do your weekly plan, you review each working file project plan and choose the tasks to do in the new week. You don't have to figure out over and over again what needs to be done on the project, because that part of your planning has already been done. You'll have turned your weekly planning into an efficient and speedy process that actually accomplishes what it's intended to do.

A sample project plan is shown in Figure 5.5.

## CRITERIA FOR PROJECT PLANNING

Some criteria you can use to determine if work you need to do falls into the category of project planning are:

- It is complex.
- It seems difficult.
- It involves several staff.
- It is a new activity.
- There are critical deadlines.
- You are coping with changes.

## IMPLEMENTATION MAPPING

At times you will need to give thought to the design of a project plan before you can work out the implementation steps. Implementation mapping (Figure 5.6) helps identify the critical elements in the project plan, generating pertinent ideas in a free-flowing process, triggering thoughts that otherwise might lie hidden.

| Sample Project Implementation Plan | | | | |
|---|---|---|---|---|
| **Project Title:** Office Procedures Manual | | | | |
| **Objective:** To develop office procedures that have the support of management and staff by the first half of this year. | | | | |
| **Actions** | **Estimated Hours** | **People Involved** | **Target Date** | **Actual Completion Date** |
| 1. Collect current procedures. | 2 | Assistant | 1/15 | |
| 2. Establish task forces to review current procedures and needed changes. | 4 | Self | 1/20 | |
| 3. Task forces review procedures and submit recommendations.* | 1 | Task force | 2/5 | |
| 4. Read and synthesize recommendations. | 3 | Self | 2/15 | |
| 5. Review by legal counsel. | | Counsel | 2/20 | |
| 6. Circulate draft for comment by managers. | | Readers | 3/1 | |
| 7. Make final edits. | 3 | Self | 3/5 | |
| 8. Oversee production.* | 1 | Assistant | 3/15 | |
| 9. Write project plan for internal PR campaign to encourage use. | 1 | Self | 3/20 | |
| 10. Distribute manual. | 2 | Assistant | 4/20 | |
| Due Date: 5/1 | | | | |
| *Those assigned task should each develop their own project implementation plan to break this task down. | | | | |

**Figure 5.5** Sample project implementation plan.

The key elements of implementation mapping are:

- Brainstorm about all elements of the task.
- Identify the critical elements to success.
- Group ideas into categories.
- Incorporate these into an implementation plan.

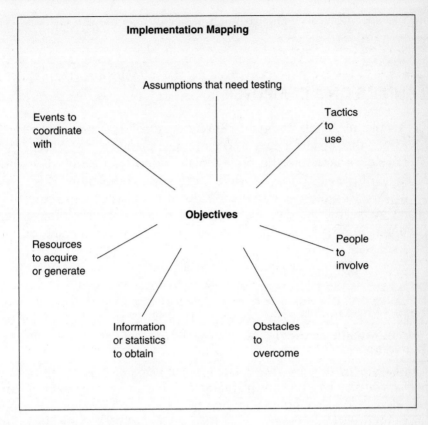

**Figure 5.6**    Implementation mapping.

## Planning in Microsoft Outlook/Lotus Notes

Both Outlook and Lotus Notes provide the possibility to do project planning within the Outlook and/or Lotus Notes environment.

You can easily create a task list within Outlook or Lotus Notes that integrates with the calendar. By creating a new category with the name of the project and following this, a list of tasks with deadlines noted in the calendar, you have a wonderful tool to use to keep track of your project plans.

You are able to look at these tasks through the calendar view if scheduled, as well as look at all open tasks by viewing through the category.

The advantage is obvious. Integration with the calendar and being able to link to e-mail messages as well as documents regarding the plan into the specific tasks make it much easier to execute the tasks when the time arrives.

## PLANNING ON A COMPUTER

I do my planning on a computer. I use a personal information software application that makes it easy to do a project plan.

I can add a task into the project plan, along with a due date and the name of the person responsible for the task completion. This way, I only have to write the information down once, yet I can retrieve it several ways—by due date, by project plan designation, by the name of the person responsible, or whatever way is most convenient for me at the moment.

I can do my weekly plans quickly by scrolling through my complete task list and assigning those I will work on in the next week to a "Weekly Plan" category. It is this weekly plan category that I view constantly. As I write this, for example, my computer is tracking 1,568 tasks I have to do. I know that because the computer tells me that's how many tasks I have to do.

Already some of you may be digging your heels in, ready to resist the idea of using a computer for planning and managing your work. I can honestly tell you, though, that in the years ahead you'll either make the maximum use of computers or die professionally. We have to learn to see a computer as a tool (just as a pen or pencil is a tool) and realize that we can control and monitor and produce much better with a computer than without. No doubt, you would agree that technology is having a profound effect on our personal and professional lives and will continue to do so. You cannot expect to see the possibilities technology might bring to you and your business unless you *use* technology. You will find that using technology to plan will not only encourage more and better planning, it will also enable you to see more ways to incorporate technology into your business.

Again, why all this trouble? Because we all want to succeed. In the book *Think and Grow Rich* (Fawcett Crest, 1960), Napoleon Hill studied Andrew Carnegie, Henry Ford, and others. One of the common denominators shared by these successful people was that they were meticulous planners. They each knew what they wanted to accomplish, took the time to figure out how to accomplish their goals, and then worked until they did exactly that. It's a model we all need to follow.

## Microsoft Outlook/Lotus Notes Calendaring

Microsoft Outlook and Lotus Notes calendaring functions are very robust. The calendaring functionality allows for the scheduling of routine tasks and repeated work, providing a better overall view of planning because of the ability to view planning in many different ways. These applications provide for audible appointment reminders.

You can link tasks as well as attachments to the calendars. What's more, in many companies it is possible to view other people's calendars through both applications, which would obviously be impossible with a paper calendaring system. This is especially helpful when you are trying to set up meetings among various individuals.

## STRATEGIC PLANNING

With a daily, weekly, and project plan we have identified the tactical steps necessary to get things done. But the question remains, are you getting the things done you should be getting done? Have you chosen the right projects to do? Do you have the long-term view in mind? Are the projects based on a sound assessment of where you should be headed? Are they the efforts that will get you where you want to go in the most effective and efficient way? Do you have the resources to carry out these grand plans or could the resources be used more wisely?

Strategy is all wrapped up in goals and, finally, what is important to the business or you. Without a clear long-term vision, whatever you may be able to get done in a day or week, a year, or a lifetime may not get you very far or be all that valuable.

How do you develop a strategy? This is easily the subject of a book on its own. First you must establish the goals you wish to attain. These goals will be driven by your vision and your customers' needs. (More on this later in this chapter under "Goals" and "Values.") Where are you now in respect to these goals? How do you get from where you are now to where you want to go? What resources do you have to work with (finances, people, time, knowledge, experience, contacts who have solved the problems you face in accomplishing your goals, and so forth)? What is the best use of existing resources to get you to where you want to go? Give yourself a direction. Consider the vari Think your strategy through as far as you possibly can.

In some companies, the development of the strategy is part of the yearly budget process. This may be too narrow a focus. Yes, finances are a critical resource (and restraint). But financial goals and the strategic planning for achieving them comprise only one part of the process. Linking strategic review so closely to the budget process review may prevent you from seeing the value and relation of the strategic planning process to other areas of the business.

I have worked with hundreds of companies over the years and although some may have developed strategies for their business or division, few of the staff have any clue about what these strategies are. Defining the strategies to be followed and making them known allow all staff members to better align their own individual actions with the important objectives of the group.

Strategic planning, as I view it, is a tool for any job level. Any objective or goal should have a strategy developed for its accomplishment. The overall strategy of the activity should be used to guide the individual in the development of his or her own strategies. With a good strategy in place, establishing the priorities to be worked on is easy. Establishing the ingredients—what working files need to be created and which of these working files requires a project—is also much easier. The question now becomes, what to strategize?

> *If you don't know where you are going, any road will get you there.*
> —Unknown

## GOALS

Strategies are built around goals. If you have not set final objectives (goals), how could you know what would even be an appropriate strategy?

Goals could be defined as broad objectives or aims, to which end efforts and actions are directed.

There are qualitative differences between goals. To try out for and make the high school tennis team is a goal but doesn't hold quite the same significance as an ultimate goal to help others by contributing to the discovery of the cause of cancer and be remembered for it for all time. Ultimate goals—those lifetime objectives that define purpose and provide meaning—will be covered in subsequent sections.

Goals are important because once they are established they focus attention and increase concentration. Focused attention and concentration result in more productivity—more of the important things being done.

Goals must be well defined, preferably worked out in writing. Writing forces you to clarify your thoughts.

Identifying and setting goals is a critical part of the PEP planning process. As a salesperson, you may have financial goals such as to make a certain amount in commissions during the year. You may have other goals as well: to become a sales manager, to reach the top 1% of all sales personnel, and so on. Each would have to be identified, have a strategy designed, have project plans written, and be followed through on a weekly and daily basis.

You likely will have a number of roles you play in your work. Marketing manager, chairman of the credit committee, XYZ board member, team leader—these can all be considered staff roles you play. Each role may have its own set of goals. When you see how many goals come into play, it isn't hard to see why people may have difficulty achieving them, particularly if they lack a process or system to accomplish their goals.

Identify the various roles you play in your job and work out your goals for each role (clear these goals with those you work with and for).

*The greater danger for most of us is not that our aim is too high and we miss it but that it is too low and we reach it.*
—**MICHELANGELO**

## PERSONAL GOALS

We've all known someone who talked on and on about some fantasy, such as giving it all up and moving to Tahiti. Suppose a person fantasizes for years about moving to Tahiti, but it isn't meant to be. It is too expensive; the individual never has the time or money; or a job and/or personal responsibilities eat up every moment of his or her life. It's sad that so many people live their lives without realizing their dreams.

At least in this example, the person had a dream, but the dreamer didn't know how to achieve it. Maybe it was too overwhelming. Or maybe the dream was too dreamlike—it never became a clearly defined goal where objectives could be identified and set against real time.

Personal happiness is in no small part wrapped around setting and working on personal goals.

In my work. I find that people more often set professional goals, either because they are imposed by the boss or because life has taught them that if they do not have a pretty clear idea of what they need to accomplish in their job they will fail to perform what they are being paid to do. The same discipline is not generally applied to one's personal life. That's a shame because, obviously, there is more to life than work.

To get clarity on your personal goals, use Stephen Covey's suggestion in *The 7 Habits of Highly Effective People* (Simon & Schuster, 1989) and define your private roles: mother, sister, wife, head of the Parent-Teacher Association, artist, best friend, and so on. It is likely that each of these roles will have one or more inherent goals. Some goals will be more important than others. Some are short-range; some are lifetime goals. Once you begin this process you see that life is rather complex. Just keeping track of your goals is a major accomplishment! We are not even talking about the hundreds of details involved in reaching them.

Whether personal or professional, goals function like directional lights. They shed light on overriding objectives and provide us a reason to develop strategies. Still, we need to know that our goals are important and meaningful. What your goals are depends on what you value.

## VALUES

While most business is conducted to create profit, long-term success requires more than achieving that one goal. For example, you might improve current profit by eliminating investment toward the future or by cutting costs to the detriment of customer service, but either activity could mean the death of the business.

It is the responsibility of the top executives to define what is truly important to the business. This is not some public relations (PR) exercise. It is a serious strategic step. What is the reason for the existence of your business? What principles does the business live by? What is your organizational vision? What are the governing values of the business?

Often a company defines its purpose and principles in a one-page mission statement and invites employees to develop goals and objectives in alignment with it.

As a manager you might call together your management team to delineate the most important issues your department, group, or business is facing, where you want the business to be in the next several years, and what might prevent you from being there. You might involve all of your staff in the process. The end result would be agreement on the most important issues to deal with so business and professional goals can be met.

## VALUES ON A PERSONAL LEVEL

One of the most important questions you need to answer for yourself is, "What truly matters to me?" If you have not identified the principles you value and wish to live by, it will be very hard to work out your purpose in life. But if you do determine what your principles are—those ideals that you value above all else—your purpose or mission in life becomes all the more clear. If you know what is important to you, you can then establish goals to realize it. These goals will be meaningful, because achieving them will give you what you truly value.

There is tremendous strength in this approach. Charles R. Hobbs, the author of the book *Time Power* (Harper & Row, 1987), calls this self-unification:

> *When what you do is in congruity with what you believe, and what you believe is the highest of truths, you achieve the most gratifying form of personal productivity and experience the most satisfying form of self-esteem. (p. 21)*

By establishing your most vital priorities in life you can achieve what Hobbs describes as a concentration of power: "the ability to focus on and accomplish your most vital priorities."

Establishing your values isn't a glib exercise. You're reading this book because you appreciate how valuable time is. You no doubt want more control of it. You want to be able to make better use of it. It would be a shame to come to the end of your life and realize you had not done and been what you wanted to do and be.

Dr. Wayne Dyer, in his audiotape series *Real Magic,* talks of his experiences working in a hospital with terminally ill patients. He noticed that no one ever regretted not having spent more time in the office. The regrets were about the handling of relationships or time with loved ones.

Don't wait until it's too late to realize you have spent the bulk of the time of your life on things that were not the most important to you. It's far better to analyze your goals, your beliefs, and your guiding principles and to make sure your work is in alignment with them.

Most of us want happiness in life. But what brings it about? Happiness is a by-product of working and living with meaning and purpose. Establishing goals based on one's values provides that meaning and a purpose for living. The beauty of working toward the accomplishment of a goal is that it almost doesn't matter whether you achieve the goal—the fact that you are working toward things that matter to you is enough to bring you happiness. Even the most mundane of actions becomes tolerable, even enjoyable, because you know it's leading you closer to the accomplishment of your goals.

If you're to do the things that are most important to you in life, you will need to manage your time wisely:

- Decide what you value above all else.
- Decide what principles you wish to live by.
- Identify your mission in life.

> *The purpose of life is a life of purpose.*
> —ROBERT BYRNE

## VISUALIZATION—WHAT YOU SEE IS WHAT YOU GET

You're most likely familiar with the concept of visualizing desired results before the actual performance. Athletes have employed the technique for years. Visualization means crossing the finish line in your mind's eye or imagining the perfect dive. Everything slows down, and you're aware of all that is happening. You see yourself making that three-point basket in the final game of the NBA championship playoffs just as the buzzer sounds to win the game. Charles Garfield, a research psychologist, has spent many years studying hundreds of world-class athletes. In his book *Peak Performance: Mental Training Techniques of the World's Greatest Athletes* (Warner Books, 1984), he says:

> *All peak performers I have interviewed report that they use some form of mental rehearsal in both training and competition.*

How important is organizational vision? Jim Clemmer, in his book *Firing on All Cylinders* (Irwin Professional Publishers, 1992), writes:

> *Your organizational vision acts as a magnet. It attracts people, events, and circumstances to it. Another way of looking at visioning*

*is as a self-fulfilling prophecy. What your people believe will happen, they will make happen, often unconsciously.*

We've spoken of action following clarity of picture. The planning process described in this chapter allows you to get that clarity of picture. There is a difference between dreaming about having something in the future and *visualizing* having it in the future. Visualizing implies a more structured and disciplined view of what you are trying to accomplish. By visualizing, you look at your goal from many different viewpoints. By examining your work from all of the viewpoints described here, you get clarity and act on the things that are the most important and will result in the greatest payback.

By dreaming and visualizing (prompted by a good planning process), you create more reasons to want what you are looking at and you increase your desire for it. Want and desire, in no small part, determine whether you accomplish what you set out to do.

The Japanese are known for the speed by which they can bring a new product to the market. Yet they also have a reputation for taking a long time to decide. This has been incorrectly labeled as a Japanese process of consensus building. Yes, they build consensus. But they also make sure that every angle has been thoroughly looked at before they begin. And once they begin, they act with blinding speed.

You must go through this thorough process if you are to act in the most effective way. The planning process prompts you to examine your work from many points of view. You identify the objects that comprise the objective—the work. The work is categorized in many additional ways it might not otherwise be if you neglected thorough planning.

You must be well organized to execute this all-essential planning process efficiently. You don't necessarily want to spend a lot of time on it. You want to spend the majority of time getting the actions done. But the time and effort are worth it. When you learn to plan most effectively, you'll discover that you are spending some part of every day visualizing and, better yet, actualizing your goals with this process.

## FOLLOW-UP FOR CHAPTER 5

**1.** Commit to a daily and weekly action plan. With practice, an analysis of your work for the coming week should take you two to four hours on Friday and probably less if you computerize the process. Devote 10 minutes or so to a daily action plan each morning of the workweek and track your progress through the workday. Your daily planning will be much simplified if you work backward from the larger picture of a weekly plan and derive your daily to-do lists from a series of tasks designed to move you closer to a larger goal.

**2.** Go through all of your sources of work as part of your weekly action plan. Prioritize these various items and plan out your week. Eliminate multiple sources by combining any stray notes into one list. Use these current notations, along with items in your pending box and tickler file, to create your weekly list.

**3.** Remember to allow sufficient time in your planning for unplanned or unidentified work.

**4.** Remember to define the key objectives to be accomplished. Break down these objectives into smaller tasks. Once a week, review these activities and use them to help create a weekly action plan for yourself. These projects should be counted among your sources of work identified in step 2.

**5.** Define what is important to the business in the long term. Where do you want the business (or your portion or area of responsibility) to be in the years ahead? You may invite your staff to participate in this process. From this process define specifically (and in writing) what goals you will work on over a defined period of time.

**6.** Create a working file for each goal.

**7.** Establish a strategy for the accomplishment of each goal.

**8.** Write project plans covering the tactical steps necessary to accomplish the strategies.

**9.** Do some soul-searching. Consider those values you hold to be most important to you. Stephen Covey cleverly suggests you imagine attending your own funeral. What would you hope would be said in a eulogy? In your life, what have you done that you are most proud of? And at the end, what would you hope to have accomplished with your life?

**10.** Remember, having a purpose in life provides meaning. What is your purpose in life? If you do not know, or it is unclear, work to identify it. Some call identifying it their mission statement.

**11.** Work out the immediate goals that contribute most to your purpose or mission in life.

**12.** Apply the PEP planning process to these goals:

Strategy.
Project plans.
Weekly/monthly planning time.
Daily plans.

Good luck!

Re: About the meeting

# Dealing with E-mail Now! The Single Biggest Challenge for Most People

# Chapter 6 Preview

In this chapter you will learn:

- The best way to process large amounts of e-mail and information is to not get it in the first place!
- To set standards for the different types of communications you send and receive.
- How to process information more efficiently.

Based on our own client experiences, I can say the single greatest source of overwhelm and stress people experience at work comes from the volume of information they are expected to process. The torrent of information comes from many sources. The most abused of these is e-mail—and not only corporate e-mail. Many e-mails now come from brand-new sources including social and business networking sites like LinkedIn and Facebook. And let's not forget the text messages being forwarded from cell phones and instant messaging (IM) services.

Reuters, some years ago, conducted a study (1,300 managers were interviewed in the United Kingdom, United States, Hong Kong, and Singapore) that identified for the first time how information overload contributes to stress. Two out of three respondents associated information overload with tension with colleagues and loss of job satisfaction; 42% attributed ill health to this stress; 61% said that they have to cancel social activities as a result of information overload, and 60% reported that they are frequently too tired for leisure activities.

So, it is not a stretch to say people seem to be in a chronic state of mental overload. The many information sources create distractions that are difficult for people to overcome or work through. According to a recent study by the Radicati Group, a Palo Alto market research firm, the average corporate e-mail user gets 127 e-mails per day, up 51% from 2003.

> **The Journal of Experimental Psychology** *found it takes your brain four times longer to recognize and process each thing you're working on when you switch back and forth among tasks.*
>
> —JULIE MORGENSTERN, *Never Check E-mail in the Morning* **(Simon & Schuster, 2004)**

Carl Honore, journalist and author of *In Praise of Slowness,* says knowledge workers can expect only three minutes of uninterrupted time before being interrupted! But, on average, it takes between eight and eleven minutes to get back to what you were doing when distracted from a piece of work. Eight to eleven minutes may be too little. Professor Georges of N.E.T Research, an authority on the working environment, says, "It takes as much as twenty minutes of undisturbed brainpower before the brain is once again capable of optimally using the frontal lobes."

Mary Czerwinski, a computer scientist at Microsoft who studies how computers affect human behavior, says knowledge workers constantly move from one task to another "like bees in a rose garden." Her studies show that, when dealing with an interruption, many of us move to a new task 40% of the time, rather than return to the original task. According to her research, it takes 25 minutes to move through all the subsequent interruptions and finally return to what you were doing in the first place.

Furthermore, researchers at King's College, London University, reported that the IQ scores of workers who were tested when subjected to distraction and overload dropped an average of 10 points. On the other side of the coin, when some companies banned e-mail on Fridays, they reported increased productivity and a reduction of e-mail by up to 75%, even on days other than Friday.

No doubt most of us suffer from information overload: too much e-mail, too many demands coming at us from too many places. And the result is a much more difficult working environment.

Although e-mail is likely the main culprit, cell phones, BlackBerrys, PDAs, IMs, and open office architecture all create an environment conducive to distractions, making it difficult to focus on what people are really optimally being paid to do.

This chapter is broken down into two main sections. The first section provides tips and ideas on how to help you prevent getting too much information in the first place. The second section covers how to process, in a more efficient and effective way, all the e-mail and other information that comes across your desk and through your computer.

## PART ONE: TAKE CONTROL OF WHAT YOU GET

First of all, there is no easy way around this particular problem. We are often at the mercy of the people working around us. Even if you have high ambitions to gain control over the number of e-mails and the amount of information you receive, you will certainly find people you are working with who are not willing to cooperate with your initiative.

Furthermore, no matter how conscientious you are about organizing your work methods and processes, you have an uphill battle on your hands. There will always be interruptions. There will be days when the inbox overflows. There will be emergencies that knock out your plans. Don't despair. Do not let setbacks take you off course. Keep exerting order and control, and you will gradually gain it.

Your first action is to catch up with overdue mail and communications and set up an electronic organization structure that makes it easy for you to find things and act in a timely way. (See Chapter 3, "Steps to Organize E-Mail," page 65.) Once you are organized and caught up, test out some of the following ideas, and see if you can tame this beast.

## The More E-Mail You Send, the More You Will Receive

If you send a lot of e-mail, you can expect to receive a lot of e-mail. If you want to cut down on the amount of e-mail you receive, cut down on the amount of e-mail you originate. Be more selective about the e-mails you send and what they contain, and you will find that you can control, to some degree, the amount of e-mail you receive. One of our IBT offices in Europe advises clients to allow e-mail threads to only go to three levels: origination, reply, reply, and then stop. If something is so complex that it requires a high degree of clarification or information exchange to make a decision, then it is probably something best suited to a simple telephone call, or maybe, a brief one-on-one meeting.

## Push to Pull

Some companies have cut down e-mail considerably by establishing a company-wide portal, where information that would otherwise have been delivered by e-mail can be posted, allowing people to access it at their discretion, instead of having to process every e-mail. Posting information for others shifts the communication from being pushed to the recipient to being pulled by the readers at their convenience.

These companies have found that posting meeting minutes and action points on such an intranet team page cut down considerably on the use of e-mail to collaborate around a project, meeting, or activity.

## If You Have Administrative Support

In the good old days (not so long ago), many of us were blessed with having a personal assistant or secretary. The assistant typically would gather all of the mail, sort and filter unnecessary information, and categorize it to be processed by the manager. If you have administrative support, that person should continue to do this, but you can have your assistant help you with your electronic information in other ways as well. Obviously, having phone calls go to the assistant or secretary, instead of to you, provides one sort of buffer.

I have seen managers have their support staff deal with the com-munications that come across their desks in more robust ways. One manager would set aside time with his assistant so that he could pro-cess his e-mail verbally, while she took notes on the things she could follow up on or compose answers to. He was able to dictate instructions that she could process much more quickly than he would have been able to otherwise. She soon learned the kinds of things the manager did not need or want to see, and was able to filter these things out, whether they came through voice mail or e-mail.

Unfortunately, not all of us are blessed to have such an assistant. You can do other things to filter the information you get.

## Technical Solutions

It is a common practice for Internet service providers (ISPs), online pub-lications, and web sites to sell your personal information to marketers. You know this by the spam you receive in your inbox. Most companies have fairly robust spam-filtering software. You can also purchase many applications for your own private PC that can prevent you from receiv-ing spam. Most ISPs have improved their spam-filtering technologies, and spam may not be quite the problem it has been in recent years. Nevertheless, it is still an irritating waste of time to receive marketing materials you do not want.

One method to cut down on the amount of spam you receive is to not sign up for mailing lists when you go to an Internet site. If you're already on such lists, unsubscribe.

Much of the spam that somehow gets past other filters comes with similar words that can be tagged for filtering. By using rules and alerts in Microsoft Outlook and Lotus Notes, you can establish guidelines by which e-mail will be sent into a specific folder instead of into your inbox. Spam can be directed to the delete folder so that you don't see it in the first place. Establishing a rule such as "any e-mail received with the word 'Viagra' in the subject or text automatically goes into the delete folder" is an easy process.

Another recent (unsavory) development in some companies is calen-dar spam. Spammers send "meeting invitations" that show up directly in your calendar. Calendar spam comes in the form of e-mail but gets posted not in the inbox, but on your calendar. In some cases, because of technical limitations, there may be no simple way to prevent this type of spam. If it becomes a real problem for you, have your administrator set up filters to turn away all meeting invitations that come from outside your company's domain.

Finally, don't forget cell spam. More and more of us are becoming the victims of it. Once again, there may be some technical solutions to control at least some of it. If it happens to you, consider:

- Go to your cell account online, access your e-mail and messaging preferences, and activate settings that block messages coming over the Internet.
- Register your cell telephone to block telemarketers. (In the United States, use the National Do Not Call registry, www.donotcall.gov.)
- Be wary of free downloads. Never download to your phone anything from a source you do not know.

### Change E-Mail Address

If you have a web site, you might consider changing the contact e-mail address from your personal one to info@[your domain name].com. Any inquiries from your web site will go into this e-mail account, and you can selectively process those e-mails.

### You Decide When to Handle Your E-Mail

The "rules and alerts" features of the most popular e-mail programs can do more than just eliminate spam. You can set them up so that the CCs of any e-mail would go into a CC folder to be read at another time. If your company sends daily reports on projects, products, activities, or other information that you don't necessarily need to see every day, you can establish a rule to send these into a folder and use the calendar to set a recurring reminder to prompt you to look at the folder for anything new that comes in. So, rules and alerts not only help block things you don't want to see, they can be set so you selectively process what comes into your inbox at a certain time and under circumstances you dictate.

> *Email has given us a ten-fold increase in our work and a*
> *one-hundred-fold decrease in our ability to pay attention.*
> —ART KLEINER, *Who Really Matters* (Doubleday, 2003)

## CCs and "Reply All"

It is useful to go through all of the e-mail that you receive as a CC. Do you need to see this mail? Could you request that senders take you off of their CC lists? Can you use rules and alerts to have certain CCs go into a folder to be looked at during a more appropriate time? Be selective about who you include on the CC line of an e-mail and rigorously pursue ways to get yourself off the CC lines of others.

As a general principle, avoid the use of "Reply All" on e-mails you receive, unless everyone on the list genuinely needs to see your reply. Instead, be selective about whom you include in any return reply.

## PART TWO: MANAGING AND PROCESSING INFORMATION EFFICIENTLY

Now that you have cut down on unnecessary and unwanted communications, your next step is to handle what you do get efficiently and effectively.

## Add-In Applications for E-Mail Programs—Organize Information

There are a number of new add-in software programs that can enhance Microsoft Outlook and Lotus Notes, as well as Google and Yahoo mail functionality. Using software like Boxbe (www.boxbe.com), you can set up an approved list of people from your contacts, and specific folders you choose, to scan for addresses (they refer to this as your guest list). Then, the program sorts and filters your e-mail to make certain you are receiving e-mail only from people you've specified. Boxbe creates a "Boxbe Waiting List" folder for messages from guests not yet approved.

Xobni (www.xobni.com) is another add-in program that focuses on ease of finding e-mail. When a new e-mail arrives, the sender's full communication history appears in a sidebar, including past conversations, attachments, and contact details. Xobni has an instant search function, where the e-mail and people you're looking for pop out immediately, as you type.

ClearContext (www.clearcontext.com) is an add-in that extends Microsoft Outlook capabilities to automatically prioritize, organize, and manage e-mail, tasks, and appointments. I use this application. The program automatically analyzes incoming e-mail and highlights the most important new messages in the inbox, while screening unwanted messages out of the inbox. This includes the ability to unsubscribe from unwanted conversations that occur as a result of group e-mails or distribution lists, preventing responses from cluttering the inbox. With a single click, ClearContext converts e-mails into connected tasks or appointments. These items are linked together to provide a context for all activity within an e-mail conversation. ClearContext can also defer messages to be handled at a later date; much like a snooze button for e-mail. You can then selectively batch the handling of e-mail. The add-in automatically categorizes and files related e-mail conversations, keeping messages from the same e-mail thread grouped together. All messages related to a single project, both incoming e-mails and replies, are automatically filed to the appropriate folders. ClearContext provides an integrated view of all e-mails, attachments, contacts, tasks, and appointments related to each project.

## Setting Standards

Besides Push-to-Pull and Friday e-mail bans, other corporate-wide initiatives can make a big difference in the volume and processing of communications and information. The first is the establishment of standards: When do I use e-mail? When do I use the phone?

E-mail should be responded to within a 24-hour period. E-mail is not a medium of choice to set up an appointment in five minutes. If everyone understands that e-mail is to be responded to within 24 hours, they will also understand that if something needs to be done in the next few minutes, they will either make a phone call or deal with it face to face. The phone should be used for a quicker response. Something that might take a minute or two over the phone can take 15 to 20 minutes when composing an e-mail.

Depending on the corporate policy, paperwork arriving by way of traditional mail is something that should normally be processed within a 48-hour period.

By establishing company-wide standards on when to use a particular communication vehicle, e-mail will be reduced and people will be able to get done what they need to get done in the time set aside for it.

And as mentioned earlier, standards should be established on when to CC someone and when to use "Reply All" (very seldom!)

## More Standards

- The subject of the message should be clearly noted on the subject line.
- There should only be one subject per e-mail message.
- For subject topics requiring action, use the abbreviation For Your Action (FYA).
- For e-mail messages requiring only that they be read, note For Your Reading (FYR).
- For general information, note on the subject line For Your Information (FYI).

## Processing Information

Bouncing between tasks, e-mail, telephone calls, IMs, people, and other interruptions makes the processing of work much more difficult to do. The best way of working is doing like tasks at the same time in an undisturbed, quiet environment. That may be too much to ask for, but strive to achieve it.

It is vital to apply the *Do It Now* principle when processing e-mails, the same as with paper, voice mail, faxes, IMs, and so on. Many of the problems you experience in coping with the volume of information you receive will be resolved by simply doing it now. But *when* to *Do It Now* is important.

My first suggestion is to only look at and process e-mail two or three times a day. If you feel compelled to look more often, okay. But keep in mind two rules of thumb. Establish routine times you will look at your e-mail and when you look, complete all e-mail following the four-D method below. When you look at it during your scheduled time, you don't just look at it, but you process it through to completion and empty your inbox. To begin, schedule time in your calendar to process your e-mail. You may need to adjust the times that you schedule for it, and you may need to adjust the amount of time you allot to it, based on your experiences.

Even if your corporate culture demands a more frequent response, do not look at every e-mail as it comes in. If you are in the middle of doing something else, such as updating a spreadsheet or writing a memo, finish what you are doing and only then look at and process the recent messages.

To help you gain more control, turn off all new e-mail notifications and alarms. Selectively activate your IM function. Use voice mail. You decide what gets done when. But remember, if you decide something is to be done at a certain time, *do it then!*

## The Four Ds

Remember when I say process, I don't mean look at the e-mails and decide to respond to them later. I mean complete it now. If it is not possible to complete it, take it as far as you possibly can, and set a reminder to follow through on any actions that may still be needed. If the e-mail represents a large block of work time, schedule it into your calendar and file the message away. Programs such as Microsoft Outlook let you do this simply by clicking and dragging the e-mail into your calendar function and assigning a date and time.

You can do only four things with an e-mail:

1. *Do it now!*
2. *Delegate it.* Send it to the right person to execute. Set a reminder to yourself to follow up if you don't hear back in a reasonable amount of time.
3. *Designate it.* If it's an e-mail that will take you 30 minutes or more to respond to, drag it into your task list or calendar, and set a reminder to prompt you to do it when you need to do it.
4. *Discard (or file) it.* Delete the e-mail if you don't need to keep a copy. File it if you need it for your records.

By establishing the four Ds in the processing of your e-mail, you will discover you can gain much better control over the time spent on e-mail.

Not all of us are prepared to have a work style involving emptying our e-mail box daily. For those who feel that prioritization of their messages and organizing or sorting their messages within the inbox are the best way to work, tools exist to facilitate this.

Most e-mail applications allow for changing the fields in which you view your e-mail, permit sorting from these fields and the use of colors to distinguish who you are receiving an e-mail from. You can establish a field or a color code for your boss, so that any time an e-mail comes from him or her, it sorts to the top of your inbox tree, allowing you to assign it the highest priority. If crunched for time, you can simply apply the four Ds to your boss's e-mail and at least empty that section out, and then get on to something that may be important.

## Turn Off Notifications

Most e-mail applications provide the option of a visual or audible notification when you receive an e-mail. I strongly suggest that you deactivate the notification system. You do not need to be reminded of things that you are not going to do. Turn off these irritating notifications.

## Instant Messages

Some companies have embraced instant messages (IMs), while others have not. Instant messages could substitute for e-mail if used to notify you that someone is in their office and can be contacted directly. Instant messages are sometimes useful to quickly establish a time or date for a meeting. If all participants are online at the moment, they can quickly agree to a date or time to meet to discuss something.

IMs are not for discussions. They should be used to pass quick information back and forth and then end. If the IM takes you into a discussion, stop it, and ask if you can speak in person or on the phone.

## Pending Folder

As mentioned earlier, some people keep all of their e-mail in their inbox and use the Search function to manage it. I believe everyone, even people using Search, should create a "pending" folder under the inbox hierarchy. *Pending,* by definition, is something that requires a response or action from someone else before you can act. You don't need to be constantly reminded of what you cannot do. Instead of leaving such an e-mail in the inbox as a reminder, drag it to a pending folder. If you send out e-mail that you need to follow-up, you have the option of flagging it in most e-mail applications or going into your sent box and dragging the e-mail into the pending folder. If you make it a point of looking at your pending folder every day, you will have all things you need to follow up on in one place.

## Setting Reminders

If in processing your e-mail, paperwork, or other information, you need to remember to do something by or at a certain time, I have some rules of thumb I think you might find useful. Do not set a task reminder for an arbitrary time or date in the future. By freely using the Reminder function, you may make the error of setting your reminder for a time when you won't act on it. You will soon defeat the purpose of the function. My recommendation is that when you have tasks you need to do by a certain time or date, set the reminder for the Friday before the week you intend to do the task. By setting it for Friday, you can evaluate the task against all of your priorities for the upcoming week when you do your weekly review and action plan. By popping up the reminder on Friday, you can decide when in the next week you want to do that task. You can assign it to a Weekly Plan category or the appropriate start and due dates. Either way, you will end up with a list for your next week's activities, including the tasks you have set for future action. They will be prioritized and planned—and be more likely to get done!

## Read Faster!

This may sound like a silly suggestion, but read faster. A reading course may help. Again, technology may be an answer. For example, RapidRead is a software application that helps you speed up your reading by increasing font size and enabling you to set the speed with which the text goes by. It works in e-mail applications and other word processing (Microsoft Word, Adobe Reader [PDFs], etc.) applications.

According to its own literature, RapidReader (www.rapidreader.com) displays the text of a document like a movie. Each word is like a frame of film placed in the center of your field of vision. You have control over your reading speed, between 100 and 950 words per minute. It displays the text you're reading in the cadence and rhythms of human speech.

## E-MAIL RULES OF THUMB

One of our clients, GlaxoSmithKline (formerly SmithKline Beecham), was kind enough to share some of their e-mail wisdom with us. I have summarized some of their ideas and added a few of our own. By using these ideas, you will save yourself heartache and extra work:

- When composing an e-mail message, make sure the subject matter on the subject line is clearly stated. Note if it's for action, information, reading, or otherwise.
- Limit yourself to one topic per e-mail message.

- Avoid the Reply All key.
- Use paragraphs and proper grammar.
- People often view an e-mail more negatively than they would a telephone call or face-to-face meeting. To avoid misunderstanding, keep sarcasm out of your e-mail.
- No off-color humor.
- Compose better messages. Use bullets for clarification. Underline those things you wish to stress.
- Do not reply to an e-mail when you are upset.
- When sending a web site address in an e-mail, always type out the full address, including www.
- List all recipients from which action is required in the "To" field and others in the "CC" field.
- If you are part of a Local Area Network, create a link to a document, rather than adding it to the message as an attachment.
- Avoid long e-mails. If a lot of text is required, create a separate document and attach it to the e-mail.
- Most e-mail applications allow for a full signature to appear at the end of an e-mail. Set it up so yours shows up.
- Activate the automatic spell check function so that e-mail leaves your office without spelling errors.
- If you find yourself creating and responding to mail with the same text, set up a form letter in Microsoft Word, and then copy and paste the text to save time.
- When sending a For Your Information (FYI) e-mail to another person, add a summary at the top stating what the person might find of interest in the e-mail so they are not required to read it all.
- Set up distribution lists in your Address Book for ease of sending e-mail.
- Avoid sending any nonbusiness e-mail.
- If you receive an attachment by e-mail that you need to keep, save it on your hard drive or server drive.
- As a result of globalization, it is best to avoid the use of acronyms, abbreviations, and jargon specific to the English language.
- If revising or adding to an existing e-mail document, make revisions in color so they are obvious to the recipient.
- If the message in the e-mail is bad news, don't send it. Instead, set up a meeting or a call.
- Get familiar with your company's e-mail retention policy. Comply with the rules and regulations as set by your company.

## IT IS NO EASY TASK!

It is certain that, in time, some clever person will come up with more workable solutions to the problem of information overload. But, for the moment we can only count on our own doggedness to minimize the effect of this never ending and increasing flow of information. Try some of the ideas here. Tweak them according to your experience. Do not let yourself get too disappointed if you fail. The only true failure would be giving up.

## FOLLOW-UP FOR CHAPTER 6

**1.** If you have not already done so, finish purging your e-mail inbox, applying the four Ds until it is completely empty. Set up your folder system so that all of your important e-mails are filed after they have been answered.

**2.** Process e-mail at selected times. For most people, two or three times a day is more than adequate. When you look at it during your scheduled time, don't just look at your e-mails, but process each one through to completion and empty your inbox. To begin, schedule time in your calendar to process your e-mail. You may need to adjust the times that you schedule for it, and you may need to adjust the amount of time you allot to it, based on your experience.

**3.** Turn off all e-mail notifications and alarms. Selectively activate your IM function. Use voice mail. You decide what gets done and when. But remember, if you decide something is to be done at a certain time, *do it then!*

**4.** Be selective about when you send an e-mail. If you want to cut down on the amount of e-mail you receive, cut down on the amount of e-mail you originate.

**5.** Learn how to use the Rules function of your e-mail application, and not only for spam. Use the function to reinforce batched handling of e-mail, phone calls, paperwork, and so on. Keep in mind, the computer is literal. When establishing a rule, be case sensitive and accurately spell the rule word.

**6.** Look into add-in applications that support your e-mail program for features that make filtering, searching, and organizing your information easier to manage.

**7.** When you have tasks that you need to do by a certain time or date, set the reminder for the Friday before the week you intend to do the task. By setting it for Friday, you can evaluate the task against all of your priorities for the upcoming week when you do your weekly review and action plan process.

**8.** Step by step, review the "E-Mail Rules of Thumb" for ways to improve your e-mail processing.

# CHAPTER 7

# Follow-Up and Follow-Through!

*When you get right down to the root of the meaning of the word succeed, you find that it simply means to follow through.*

—F. W. NICHOL

# Chapter 7 Preview

In this chapter, you will learn how to:

- Persevere; persistence is the most vital ingredient of success in life and work.
- Put the right systems in place to allow you to remember details.
- Use a calendar and other tools to follow up and follow through.
- Practice effective delegation. Unlimited growth is possible only through eliciting the support of others.

In Chapter 5, we covered how essential it is to have an efficient planning process in place if you are to realize your goals and objectives. Planning gives clarity, and with clarity, you act. By acting, you are halfway there. But how successful and effective you are will depend most on how well you stick to what you are trying to accomplish. You will face two main obstacles: yourself—will you keep working toward an objective, overcoming challenges, setbacks, failures, and disappointments until you reach it; and others—how effective will you be in getting others to do what you need them to do? To succeed, you need persistence and a system that enables and reinforces persistence. Fortunately, this is easier to accomplish than you might at first imagine.

> *Let me tell you the secret that has led me to my goal:*
> *My strength lies solely in my tenacity.*
>
> —Louis Pasteur

## PERSISTENCE

When I say stick to it, I almost literally mean it. Things get done, objectives are met, and goals are achieved most often because the person who wanted them possessed the stick-to-itiveness to make them happen. Calvin Coolidge, 30th president of the United States, said:

> *Nothing in the world can take the place of persistence. Talent will not; nothing is more common than unsuccessful men with talent. Genius will not; unrewarded genius is almost a proverb. Education will not; the world is full of educated derelicts. Persistence and determination alone are omnipotent.*

I suspect that your experience tells you this is true. Things happen because you make them happen, and/or persist until they do. Planning's relationship to persistence can best be summed up in a quote of Napoleon Hill in his book, *Think and Grow Rich* (Fawcett Crest, 1960). He says:

> *The majority of men meet with failure because of their lack of persistence in creating new plans to take the place of those which fail.*

This is the essence of the work process. Know what you want. Plan how to get it. Act on the plans. Follow up until it happens, or develop new plans to make it happen. Follow up on the new plans over and over until you achieve what you want. How well you do it is determined by how well you are organized.

By following the steps of the Personal Efficiency Program (PEP), you've become action oriented. You *Do It Now*. You've organized your work space and you have systems in place to keep it that way. You know how to set goals and plan to achieve them. These same principles must be applied to how you follow up and follow through.

> *That what we persist in doing becomes easier—not that*
> *the nature of the task has changed, but our ability*
> *to do it has increased.*
>
> **—RALPH WALDO EMERSON**

## PERSISTENCE, ROUTINES, AND HABITS—DOING WHAT YOU DON'T LIKE TO DO

> *Persistence is the direct result of habits. The mind absorbs and*
> *becomes a part of the daily experiences upon which it feeds.*
>
> **—NAPOLEON HILL**

I am a runner. I have been running for over 20 years. I have a routine. I wake up in the morning and put on my running clothes. I leave the house and run till I wake up and then return home! With few exceptions, I run every day. Why? Because I find running hard! Even after 20 years. Of course, I love running—when it's over! If it's raining outside or cold and I ask myself, "Do I feel like running?" I probably don't feel like it. So, I don't give myself a choice. I use my routine and habit to overcome any tendency I might have to not do it.

> *Good habits are the key to all success.*
>
> **—OG MANDINO, *The Greatest Salesman in the World***
> **(Bantam Books, 1974)**

I find it interesting that those who show up at the gym consistently arrive at the same time on the same days, like clockwork. Working out is no easier for them than anyone else. I know because I often hear the words when these people are working their abdominals: "This never seems to get easier!" They have a routine—same time, same place, and a variety of exercises. Sort of mindless: This is exactly what you want if you are doing physical exertion!

> *The secret of success of every man who has ever been successful—lies in the fact that he formed the habit of doing things that failures don't like to do.*
> —ALBERT E. N. GRAY, "The Common Denominator of Success"

Establishing habits and routines enables and reinforces persistence. I have brought up exercise because so many of us would like to do it regularly. We like the results, but find it hard to start or keep up.

In his inspiring speech to insurance agents given in 1940 and published in the article, "The Common Denominator of Success," Albert Gray said:

*Perhaps you have been discouraged by a feeling that you were born subject to certain dislikes peculiar to you, with which the successful people in our business are not afflicted. Perhaps you have wondered why it is that our biggest producers seem to like to do the things that you don't like to do.*

*They don't! And I think this is the most encouraging statement I have ever offered to a group of life insurance salespeople.*

*But if they don't like to do these things, then why do they do them? Because by doing the things they don't like to do, they can accomplish the things they want to accomplish. Successful people are influenced by the desire for pleasing results. Failures are influenced by the desire for pleasing methods and are inclined to be satisfied with such results as can be obtained by doing things they like to do.*

*Every single qualification for success is acquired through habit. People form habits and habits form futures. If you do not deliberately form good habits, then unconsciously you will form bad ones. You are the kind of person you are because you have formed the habit of being that kind of person, and the only way you can change is through habit.*

**Figure 7.1** We have limited random access memory.

So the secret is forming good habits. Establish a routine, and it forms into a habit. The habit makes persistence easier.

> *For it is another of Nature's laws that only a habit can subdue another habit.*
>
> —OG MANDINO, *The Greatest Salesman in the World* (Bantam Books, 1974)

## FORGET REMEMBERING

Most people I speak with take a certain degree of pride in their ability to remember "everything" that needs to be done. It is a mental game they play. While that may have been okay at one time, the pace of today's work and home life has accelerated and the volume of activities we could or should keep up with has grown so much that it is impractical to expect to keep on top of 1,000 things to do. No doubt you do remember these things to do, but it may not be at the time it's most convenient or effective, such as at three o'clock in the morning, when you sit up in bed and think, "Oh, I have to take care of [fill in the blank]. . . ." This constant thinking about, planning out, tracking everything you need to do—remembering everything you need to follow up on—simply overwhelms people.

I don't believe that you necessarily want to reinforce this ability to remember the many hundreds of details that make up your workload. Executives and managers should be more interested in forgetting about all these things they need to do. Yes, I said forgetting. What people need is the right system in place, to allow them to remember this myriad of details when, and only when, it's necessary for them to remember.

Sounds crazy? Not really.

It has been said that Albert Einstein couldn't tell you his own telephone number. When asked why, he was reported to have replied, "Why should I know it? I can always find it in the directory."

## PREOCCUPATION AND TIME

Have you ever noticed the first time you drive someplace it seems to take longer to get there than the second or third time? Have you ever considered why? The first time you drive somewhere you tend to be alert to where you are and where you are going. You are on the lookout for landmarks. "Three blocks past the pharmacy on Hilton Street" forces you to keep an eye out for the pharmacy and count the blocks. Once you have been there a few times, you can drive there hardly noticing the familiar landmarks. You get in the car and the next thing you know you are there! The sense of time has little to do with how fast you are driving. It has much more to do with where your attention is focused. Anyone driving today can agree that too many people are driving in their own mental worlds. They are preoccupied.

When you are preoccupied, time flies by. You will have experienced starting the workday only to discover it is time for lunch, and you wonder where the morning went and what you accomplished. Too often the cause of this preoccupation is our attempt to make sense of and keep up with the thousands of things we must do. It is the result of a poor planning process. It is our attempt to keep on top of all the things we must track and do, *mentally*.

I am convinced that this constant, unproductive preoccupation with all the things we have to do is the single largest consumer of time and energy, the biggest barrier to individual productivity, and the one thing we can all do something about to materially allow us to take control of our time and our work, and therefore our lives.

> *Any moment you are preoccupied is a moment you are not free to manage your time.*
> —JAMES McCAY, *The Management of Time*
> (Prentice-Hall, 1959)

## ORGANIZE EFFICIENT FOLLOW-UP SYSTEMS

All too often when I arrive at someone's desk, I find it scattered with reminders of things to do, perhaps in the form of Post-it notes spread out around the computer screen and over every imaginable surface. Even if you have a strong *Do It Now* habit, there are normally many things you can't complete at the moment for one reason or another. Accordingly, people leave themselves reminders.

However, having those reminders constantly staring you in the face isn't necessarily conducive to concentration, focus, and productivity. If these little reminders linger long enough one eventually becomes blind to them. Regularly looking at all of these reminders and consciously deciding not to do any one of them reinforces a *Don't Do It Now* habit.

Having simple and easy reminder systems (tools) in place enables you to overcome these problems and move on to your most important work.

### Paper Follow-Up

Since paper is so abundant and is one of the biggest nuisances around, let's begin by discussing how to handle paper. You know it's possible to get the papers off of your desk and "forwarded" to an appropriate time to do them. You can do this with a tickler file system that lets you schedule materials by the days of the month (1 through 31), or by months (1 through 12), according to due dates.

As we discussed in Chapter 3, simply make a reminder for yourself in your calendar, and then block out time to do the work. Put the reminder—the piece of paper you'll actually be working on—into the tickler system on the same date you scheduled in your calendar, so it will pop up on the day you scheduled for it. Put papers that are awaiting someone else's input into the tickler system. For example, if you send a letter to a customer and expect to hear back within a week, put your copy of the letter into the tickler system. After a week, your copy of the letter pops up, prompting you to get back to the customer for more follow-up. If a response has been received, the response will dictate your next step. Either way, the reminder prompts you to follow up and follow through.

One clever and successful man ran a medium-size bank using just this system. He had a tickler system numbered 1 to 31 and 1 to 12. This one follow-up tool was used and the whole management of the bank could be traced. He would assign duties and tasks to people or write down things to be done and use the tickler system to anticipate when he thought an assignment or a project could reasonably (and efficiently) be completed. When the reminder popped up at a date in the future, he followed up and followed through.

> *Great works are performed, not by strength, but perseverance.*
> —SAMUEL JOHNSON

## Logbook

Consolidating all the small tasks you need to do in one book eliminates the need for little pieces of paper littering your desk. A logbook of such items makes a useful reminder tool for the odds and ends of work that are part of everyone's day. You can use it when you suddenly remember something you need to do and want a place to write it down. Colleagues may pass by and verbally ask you to check on something and get back to them on it; the logbook gives you a place to write down the request and a means to note your follow-up, all in one.

I recommend a composition notebook, probably about 6 by $9\frac{1}{2}$ inches in size. Use a stitched book so the pages cannot be easily ripped out, not a spiral-bound notebook. In it maintain a chronological diary of activities. You should date each entry. Write big, and put straight lines between entries, so you can easily distinguish between tasks. As you complete a task, cross it out (see Figure 7.2). This lets you see what's been done and what remains to be done.

One manager ran his entire business using this one tool. Everything he needed to remember went into his personal logbook. He took it wherever he went.

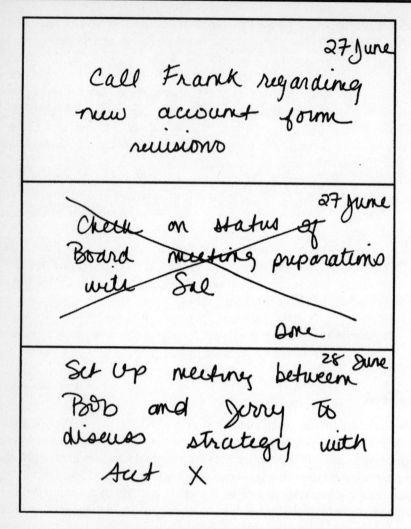

**Figure 7.2** Sample entries in a logbook.

Simply using a logbook to organize and remember things to do can be an effective reminder system, especially for secretaries. In fact, nearly all professional secretaries I have worked with have had some form of logbook.

Until you get used to writing everything down in it I recommend you always leave it open on your desk. Otherwise, chances are you will reach for the closest thing to write on and you won't develop the habit of using your logbook.

## Electronic Solutions to a Logbook

If you use a paper logbook, you know its limitations. How do you share the information in your logbook with others? How do you find information easily?

One of our European clients found a software application that substitutes well for a paper logbook. They use Microsoft OneNote. From faster search capability to ease of sharing the information, OneNote makes the management of information and tasks simpler. It can gather and organize text, pictures, digital handwriting, and audio and video recordings, all in one digital notebook on your computer. You can search and locate information not only through the Find feature or by using key words in a document, but also by searching for text within pictures or from spoken words in audio and video recordings. Meeting notes, minutes, group decisions, and brainstorming results can be posted for all to see and follow. If you are a big fan of keeping notes you may consider such software.

## Calendar Systems

Even if you use a logbook, you will always need some form of calendar system. There are many calendar systems on the market. The Franklin/ Covey Planner, Day-Timer organizer system, and Time Manager International calendaring system and course are but a few of the many calendar systems you may have seen. Each of these has a built-in philosophy of time management. These planners are excellent follow-up tools. After all, you can be reasonably sure you'll check your calendar daily, so it makes a good place to jot down items you want to remember. Because calendars are dated, they anticipate future needs, and you can use them as a sort of linear tickler file, if nothing else.

Our Scandinavian offices have designed calendar systems following the planning concepts of PEP. Like others mentioned here, this is a calendar system you can carry around with you (it fits in a small purse or suit pocket for convenience) and use to track your activities and plan your week. It has a week-at-a-glance calendar view and sections for addresses and telephone numbers, as well as other personal information.

One good rule of thumb for any calendar system is this: Whether you choose a large, deskbound calendar system with many sections and features or a simple calendar system you carry in your purse or suit pocket, use one with a week-at-a-glance feature. This will reinforce your likelihood to plan on a weekly and a weeklong basis and increase your chances of success in both scheduling and accomplishing your work.

If you're inclined to use a bigger and more sophisticated system, you might include subdivisions such as an address book section, a section for your project plans, or a section for notes you take during meetings. Learn to use your calendar system to its full potential. A little imagination, combined with the necessary training and trial and error, will show you follow-up and follow-through capabilities.

An effective calendar system helps you to:

- Remind yourself of future tasks.
- Note appointments.
- Write to-do lists or plan for the upcoming week.
- Note important deadlines.
- Work back from deadlines and note milestones.
- Remind yourself of recurring events such as birthdays, holidays, anniversaries, and other special dates in your life.
- Write notes from meetings.
- Keep address and telephone information.
- Provide general information, such as time zones, telephone area codes, and postal zip codes.
- Block out time for your own scheduled work.
- Schedule recurring activities such as time to meet employees on a weekly basis, to process your e-mail, and to do paperwork.
- Store personal information such as insurance policy numbers, driver's license number, automobile registration numbers, and so on.
- Organize activities based on your purposes and goals.

A well-used calendar for scheduling and following through on activities might look similar to the one shown in Figure 7.3.

## Electronic Solutions to Follow-Up and Follow-Through

It makes sense to me, if you have not already done so, to convert to an electronic calendaring system. Most computers come with a calendaring application of one form or another. If not, scores of personal information manager applications are available on the market, and depending on the nature of your work you are certain to find one that suits your needs. Organizing yourself with one of these applications is fast and flexible. Instead of the tedious and sometimes time-consuming

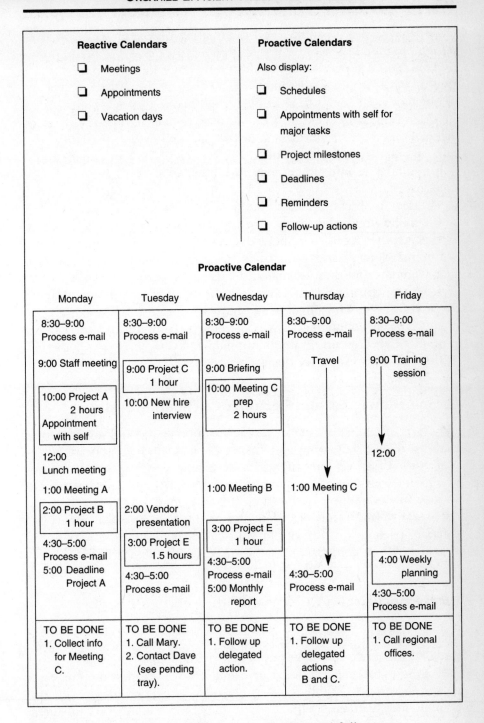

**Figure 7.3** Sample calendar for scheduling and follow-up.

efforts that go into planning and calendaring on paper, a good calendaring program lets you use your computer to jot down or revise things quickly. You can plan reminders for future dates that will automatically pop up at the appropriate time.

Much of what comes to us in the form of work arrives as e-mail. It's a quick and simple process to drag and drop e-mails into your task list or calendar and to set reminders to act on them when you intend to act.

If you send out e-mail instructions, you can "flag" an e-mail, and it will remind you in a timely way to follow up if you have not had a response.

The search function makes finding items much easier and faster.

Computers come in many forms and serve many functions. From BlackBerrys to Treos, handheld devices now combine multiple functions, including phone, e-mail, text messaging, calendaring, and task management. One big advantage in using these devices is that they typically synchronize with your desktop or laptop computer. Having all of your critical information in one easy device offers a big advantage. Your set reminders follow you wherever you are, and you can act promptly to follow up on important matters. (Chapter 9 covers the use of these devices in greater detail.)

## Combination Paper and Electronic Calendaring Systems

Although I usually encourage people to embrace technology and computerize their calendaring systems, some may find that computerization doesn't fit their type of work. For example, going to a lunch appointment with a laptop computer may be a bit much. Many people successfully combine paper and electronic calendaring systems, taking advantage of both. Most electronic Personal Information Manager (PIM) software packages can print out your calendar in almost any conceivable size. When going to appointments you can use a printout.

## WORK GROUPS

With the advent of network systems, it is now possible and even affordable to network nearly any group within an organization. What used to require a million-dollar investment is now within the means of most small groups. The hardware and software needed to network and communicate with each other are affordable to virtually every business.

Follow-up and follow-through are greatly enhanced in a group setting, of course, because groups can develop specific plans for a variety of projects involving any number of different people. These plans can be implemented concurrently, tracked, supervised, or merely viewed by any member of the group.

From the manager's perspective, multiple projects can be tracked with ease. You can view any one or all of the projects your direct reports are responsible for. You can also view the separate tasks and completion deadlines for any of those projects or view the separate (and multiple) tasks for more than one project simultaneously, depending on your software and hardware. This capability lets you keep track of multiple deadlines.

You can get a perspective on the work being done from the viewpoint of any of the people involved and track work that needs to be completed concurrently or prior to the completion of other assignments. You can identify problems you may have been unaware of or merely suspected. For example, if you view the task list of several of your people in columns on a single screen and you see one has an unfair or overly large task load, you may want to look again at how your office delegates.

As changes, modifications, or updates are made, everyone in the network automatically has those updates available. Information can be viewed against time and deadlines. If an individual becomes ill, it's easy to identify his or her responsibilities and tasks, and then redistribute them equitably among the other members of the group. The need for physically meeting to cover issues or plans is greatly reduced, thereby increasing the time available for actual work.

## FOLLOW-UP AND DELEGATION

Delegation determines to a large degree your effectiveness as an executive, manager, or supervisor. The quality of your work also depends on your ability to properly delegate. Proper delegation enables you to follow up and follow through effectively. If you delegate properly, you will multiply your productivity.

The sooner in your planning process that you detect overload—yours or someone else's—the more effective you will be if you correct the problem. You can't expect to do everything yourself.

*Save your time for what you do best, and delegate the rest.*
—JULIE MORGENSTERN, *Never Check E-Mail in the Morning*
(Simon & Schuster, 2004)

You can waste a lot of time trying to master something you are not very good at. Delegating properly, to the right person with the right skills, is one of the most important executive skills. When you delegate, you are assigning another person a task to do and the authority to do it, even though you do not hand over your personal accountability. That stays with you.

One of the best sources of information on the subject of delegation is the book *Don't Do. Delegate!* (Ballantine Books, 1985) by James Jenks and John Kelly. The following two lists, gleaned from this and other sources, contrast effective and ineffective delegation:

| **The Effective Delegator** | **The Ineffective Delegator** |
|---|---|
| 1. Identifies the correct person to do the job. | 1. Distributes workload arbitrarily. |
| 2. Delegates now, giving adequate time for completion. | 2. Delegates just before deadline, thereby creating crisis. |
| 3. Clearly states the objective. | 3. Does not clearly communicate the envisioned outcome. |
| 4. Provides all information needed to complete the task. | 4. Issues minimal, hurried instructions. |
| 5. Makes sure staff understands task before taking action. | 5. Delegates in a way that creates misunderstandings. |
| 6. Sets deadline for completion. | 6. Asks for everything as soon as possible. |
| 7. Encourages written project plan. | 7. Hopes staff develops an effective approach to task. |
| 8. Regularly monitors progress. | 8. Establishes no formal review process. |
| 9. Is accessible for clarification and advice. | 9. Interferes with how job is being done. |
| 10. Assumes responsibility, but gives credit to the person who did the job. | 10. Assigns blame to others if result not achieved, but takes credit if achieved. |
| 11. Helps staff grow by introducing them to new responsibilities. | 11. Doesn't delegate but instead holds on to the task and acts as a bottleneck. |

There is a more important reason to refine your skills of getting others to do the work for you. Eliciting the support of others is the only way you will achieve broad success, both personally and professionally. Only by tapping into the support of others can you multiply your output. There is a limit to any one individual's productive capacity, time, and knowledge. Skillful delegation means limitless production potential.

## DELEGATION—USING YOUR ELECTRONIC TOOLS

In some cultures how you delegate can be a sensitive topic. A large Dutch power company client experienced this. There was a negative reaction to how some people would delegate within the concern. Some staff would object to how they were being told what to do.

Our IBT office addressed the issue in this way: The company was a Microsoft Outlook user. They decided to teach all employees how to use the task list in Outlook as a way to keep track of activities without constantly having to nag the employees about the status. IBT's first action was to have the manager concerned go around and see all of the employees and inform them of the new method of tracking delegated tasks through Outlook. He stressed how much easier it would be on the employees by applying this electronic tool to manage their tasks.

Person-responsible categories were created within the Outlook task management. All tasks were assigned to the person responsible.

An additional column was added to the task list form showing the percentage of completion of the task. In this way, the manager could look at the overall list of tasks for the person responsible and the person could make a notation of how far they had progressed on the task, be it 25% complete, 50% complete, 75% complete, and so on.

The managers still had to apply the principles as previously noted but with this tool they were able to keep track of the vast majority of things that were open and outstanding in their departments without having to be overly intrusive on the employees.

The employees appreciated the fact that the managers went around and saw them and tried to take up and improve delegation procedures in the department. That in and of itself was worth the effort.

## EXCEPTIONS TO THE RULE

It can be very frustrating when you have to track down what others have done. On the other hand, if you don't track your subordinates' work, it often means failure. How you pass tasks on for others to do can affect your results. Effective delegation greatly increases your chances of success. Some people simply will not perform, so don't delegate to them. Give the job to someone else or figure out another way to get the job done.

I use an old rule of thumb. When it comes to getting something done, *give it to a busy person.* Idle people often remain idle when given things to do. Busy people—if they are effective—are busy because they are consistently and regularly working, and that's the person you want to assign tasks to.

*Next week there can't be any crisis. My schedule is already full.*
—HENRY A. KISSINGER

## MAKE FOLLOW-UP PART OF THE WORK PROCESS

*Keep on starting, and finishing will take care of itself.*
—NEIL FIORE, *The Now Habit* (Penguin, 2007)

Your weekly planning process becomes the formal time for you to get an overview of your work, look at all of your objectives and plans, prioritize your upcoming week, and remind yourself of what you need to follow up on. Scheduling your weekly planning and doing it ensures that no important item gets overlooked.

As an executive, manager, or supervisor, you should use your weekly one-to-one meeting with your direct reports as the time to follow up on the items you're tracking through to completion. By scheduling and holding these meetings regularly, you let your people know what to expect. They know it is time for progress reports and that progress is expected. It eliminates random checking and disturbing your people in the process. Your staff members, in turn, have the chance to follow up with you on input you're expected to supply. They know the meeting is predictable, useful time that helps them get their own jobs done better and faster.

If you learn to recognize the tools that exist to facilitate follow-up and follow-through and make these tools an efficient part of the work process, you'll make it much easier to persist to success.

## FOLLOW-UP FOR CHAPTER 7

**1.** How successful and effective you are primarily depends on how well you stick to what you're trying to accomplish—in other words, how well you follow up and follow through. Things happen because you make them happen, or you must persist until you do.

**2.** Adopt simple and easy reminder systems that will enable you to overcome problems and let you move on to your most important work. If you have a stack of papers on your desk that detail tasks to be done, eliminate the clutter by scheduling this work in your calendar, and filing the papers in a tickler file. Then, on the appropriate date, the papers will be there to remind you of a task to be done, and you will have blocked out the time to complete that task.

**3.** Eliminate the clutter of multiple reminders by consolidating everything into a logbook. Use it every day to reinforce the habit, and you'll keep your desk clear at the same time. Use the logbook when you suddenly remember something you need to do and you want a place to write it down. Use it to keep track of verbal requests to do things. Date each task to be done, and cross off the task when it's completed. A logbook provides a reminder system and a follow-up system all in one by prompting you to do things and verifying tasks that have been completed.

**4.** Use a calendar system that lets you plan an entire week at a time. This will reinforce your likelihood to plan on a weekly and a weeklong basis and increases your chances of success in both scheduling and accomplishing your work.

**5.** Learn not to limit the use of your calendar system. People almost never use a calendar system to its full potential. A little imagination, combined with the necessary trial and error, will show you follow-up and follow-through capabilities you never anticipated.

**6.** Do not overlook electronic solutions. If your firm uses Outlook or another group application, consider adopting it as your calendar/task management tool. Most PDAs and pocket PCs support Outlook (and other popular applications) and can be useful tools for mobile workers or for when you are out of the office.

**7.** Delegation is prime in determining your effectiveness. The quality of your work also depends on your ability to properly delegate. Delegate properly and you'll multiply your productivity. Remember, when you delegate, you are assigning another person a task to do and the authority to do it. You don't hand over control or accountability, though. These stay with you.

**8.** Make follow-up and follow-through part of the process of work. You can do this by including it as part of the weekly review process as you meet regularly with each of your direct reports. Remember, too, that these weekly meetings are the time for your staff to follow up with you on input you're expected to supply. If follow-up and follow-through work both ways, these meetings will become dependable, useful times together that will help everyone do their work better and more efficiently.

**9.** Finally, remember the keys to success: persistence, routines, and good habits. Don't give up! Use your tools (calendar, handheld devices, reminder functions, etc.), so you are reminded in a timely way to follow up on things, and when you are reminded, *act now!* Establish routines to reinforce your follow-through—for example, look at your flagged e-mail folder every day, establish a weekly review and action plan (WRAP) time and stick with it, set up a weekly one-on-one meeting with each direct report and review open issues. Make these into habits! Make persistence a habit!

# CHAPTER 8

# Do It *Right*, Now!

*You can't escape the responsibility of tomorrow by evading it today.*

—ABRAHAM LINCOLN

# Chapter 8 Preview

In this chapter, you will learn:

- It isn't enough to do what you think is important. Check what the customers' expectations are and fulfill those needs.
- To improve the process of your group's work, you should begin with the process of your personal work.
- To make dramatic improvement, you must abandon your old ways of processing your work and start using new methods to introduce more effective ways of working.

## APPLY THIS ONE PRINCIPLE, AND THAT IS ALL YOU NEED TO DO

If there is a philosophical basis for PEP, it can be defined as the application of continuous incremental improvement to the basic processes of one's work. It is how I designed the program (though I admit I didn't do it consciously!). I will cover this more in Chapter 10.

The well-known Japanese word for this process is *Kaizen*. Although *Kaizen* is broadly used in corporations, it typically addresses the major processes of the business. Since this book addresses the personal dimension, this chapter's focus will be the application of *Kaizen* to self-management.

Obviously, doing the task right the first time is common sense. It saves time. It gets the desired result. Doing it right assumes you know the technical points of your job. But doing it right also has much to do with how you process your work.

> *(How to) multiply our output: The way of self-management, a way that is well within the range of anyone who wants to grow rapidly through systematic personal effort.*
>
> —JAMES McCAY, *The Management of Time*
> **(Prentice-Hall, 1959)**

I have learned through client experiences in a score of countries that the vast majority of people are proficient and technically skilled to do their work, but they don't understand the principles of work organization or the application of these principles to their jobs.

Work process improvement is understood by most to be improvement of the computer system or manufacturing process. Most individuals are only vaguely aware of a personal work process, and they seldom, if ever, address this personal work process.

Process improvement falls under the heading of Quality. Quality initiatives, Six Sigma, Total Quality Management, 6S, Lean, and so forth, all address the same thing: process improvement. Process improvement eliminates waste. More gets done with less time, energy, and effort.

By applying the hard-won principles and techniques found in most quality programs to your personal work processes, you can realize the same benefits companies have enjoyed for decades. This chapter will detail ideas you can employ and *Do It Right Now!*

## WHY QUALITY?

The American Society for Quality (www.asq.org) has kindly provided permission to publish their arguments for Quality:

- Quality is not a program; it is an approach to business.
- Quality is a collection of powerful tools and concepts that is proven to work.
- Quality is defined by the customer through his or her satisfaction.
- Quality includes continuous improvement and breakthrough events.
- Quality tools and techniques are applicable in every aspect of the business.
- Quality is aimed at performance excellence; anything less is an improvement opportunity.
- Quality increases customer satisfaction, reduces cycle time and costs, and eliminates errors and rework.
- Quality isn't just for businesses. It works in nonprofit organizations like schools, health care and social services, and government agencies.
- Results (performance and financial) are the natural consequence of effective quality management. (Copyright © 2003 American Society for Quality. All rights reserved.)

If a leader or a manager really wants to improve the performance of his/her team, Quality initiatives are *the* answer. They are simple and effective.

## KAIZEN

*Kaizen* is arguably the single most important management concept to be applied to the manufacturing sector in the past 50 years. *Kaizen* is the Japanese word for "continuous improvement." I like to add the word "incremental"—I see the need to maintain small consistent improvements to ensure they are lasting. These improvements most directly apply to the processes involved in the work. I would therefore define *Kaizen* as "continuous incremental improvement of the process."

Applying *Kaizen* to the white-collar environment is a bit trickier than to a visible manufacturing process. Managers and service personnel have processes that are more random and harder to define. This is especially true when it comes to their personal work processes.

Yet, white-collar productivity is often very poor. Our IBT coaches find professional people, on average, waste about 50% of their time. This is not to say professional people do not work hard. They most often do. It is simply that they do not get nearly as much done as they could! How often have you arrived at the end of the day and looked at your to-do list to find only a few items done, and wondered where the day went?

I ask participants in my workshops how often they include tasks on their daily to-do list that if done would improve how they process their personal work. Seldom do people spend time on the things that would improve their work process! But when it comes to potential productivity improvement, there is no more fruitful potential than examining your own behavior in how you execute your work.

If you were to accept only this one concept from the book, and were to fully apply yourself to this concept, you could throw the rest of the book away and I would have succeeded in helping you become more organized and effective.

## PEP—A PRACTICAL TOOL FOR QUALITY IMPROVEMENT

At one division in General Motors, a client said:

> *The quality gurus build awareness here, but PEP makes time management and organizational efficiency workable because it's done on the job, at the desk, and this is practical.*

The act of improving *how* you process your work will give you visible and immediate results. The results encourage you to extend your methods to other processes and give you the fortitude to continually improve these work processes until you achieve success. It also gives you the *time* to focus on improving the broader work processes.

## 6S

A Japanese approach to the subject of quality enjoying contemporary popularity, especially among white-collar workers, is 6S. 6S is the label for:

| | |
|---|---|
| *Seiri* | Organization |
| *Seiton* | Neatness |
| *Seiso* | Cleanliness |
| *Seiketsu* | Standardization |
| *Shitsuke* | Discipline |
| *Sukam* | Habit |

6S originated in China and has been successfully copied and implemented by the Japanese. 6S as a quality process is better suited to white-collar and personal work applications.

According to Lean Affiliates, and published in their "Lean Glossary," 6S can be defined as "a set of workplace organization rules designed to increase efficiency and help enable lean manufacturing, as defined by: Sort—separate and categorize needed and unneeded materials and tools; Set in Order—arrange tools and other items for ease of use; Shine (or scrub)—maintain a high level of cleanliness; Standardize—create a systematic plan to perform the first three steps; Sustain—devise methods to turn performing the steps on an ongoing basis into a habit."

"Seiri" (Organization) can be defined as the act of sorting through the contents of your office and workspace and determining what you use for what, and what you need and don't need. Get rid of what you do not need. Eliminate the clutter. This applies to both the physical and electronic.

"Seiton" (Neatness) means having your tools where they belong, providing easy access to what you need so that you can produce. An example might be electronic documents set up so they are easy to access.

"Seiso" (Cleanliness) means keeping your work environment decluttered, neat, and orderly.

"Seiketsu" (Standards) relates to both making clear where everything is so that others can intuitively use it and establishing standards for office organization (paper and electronic files; agreed-on categories; labels; how and when to use e-mail, the telephone, and meetings; when to interrupt with a personal visit, etc.).

"Shitsuke" (discipline) means keep it up, no matter the circumstances or excuses until it becomes:

"Sukam" (Habit)—making the first listed "S" a habit!

While Chapter 2 covers the details of putting this in place, these steps reinforce the process.

Picture it this way: Have you ever seen how some chefs prepare a meal? Getting the veggies cut, peeling the potatoes, searching out the missing ingredients, preparing the salad, spicing the meat, have it all cooking away, and by the time the meal is ready the kitchen looks like it has been hit by a tornado. The meal tastes wonderful. But the cleanup is a heavy-duty chore!

Compare that scene to a visit to your local Japanese restaurant. Often, you see the Japanese chef preparing and cooking the meal. There is an art to it. As they prepare, they clean: the surface, the pans, and the knives. All ingredients have a place, with easy access, and are put back as they are used. At the time the meal is served, the kitchen is spotless. The meal takes no longer to be served. This principle can and should be applied to your work space.

Set up your workplace according to the principles of 6S. Put back the tools used as you use them. Clean up as and when you act.

6S is a way of thinking and working. 6S is being aware of the need to be efficient, being aware of waste and the need to eliminate it, spending time getting things in order, looking for ways the work can be done better and acting to make it so, and cleaning up after yourself.

The basic philosophy of 6S is to organize your materials and work space tools neatly, to execute the job in an orderly way, and to clean up afterward, so the next time you act it will be easy to do so.

The whole process (how you do what you do) needs to be addressed and improved if you are to do the right things right, now. You can do this by concentrating on the components of 6S and bringing order to your environment and the way you work.

## IDENTIFYING YOUR CUSTOMERS AND THEIR NEEDS

I run into an interesting phenomenon in delivering PEP. In conducting before-and-after surveys to establish measurements for success and to get feedback on our own work, I ask PEP participants how they have personally benefited from the program. Typically, 85% to 90% of our clients make excellent personal progress, and the results are more meaningful because they are so personal.

Another question we ask in the surveys concerns participants' perceptions of how their coworkers have done with PEP. At first the answers to this question were much more mixed. People told us, "Well, her desk isn't that clean anymore." "I still don't hear back from Sam fast enough." We found that PEP had made the participants more capable of accomplishing the things that were important to them, but they weren't necessarily meeting the needs of the people around them. Since that time, we have asked the participants to find out what their coworkers expect and need and to make the satisfaction of those needs one of their objectives. It is a great success.

The lesson to be taken from this is that it's important not only to produce what you think is important but also to produce what others perceive as important to them. You have to find out from your colleagues, coworkers, all of your "customers," both internal and external, what they consider to be important. Not only does PEP enable you to know what your customers need, being well organized enables you to respond better to those customers' needs.

> *It takes less time to do something right than it takes*
> *to explain why you did it wrong.*
> —ANONYMOUS

## WORKPLACE *KAIZEN*

In the last section you read about 6S, a process designed to improve quality and efficiency at the work space. In this section, I will elaborate on how you can use *Kaizen* in your everyday work.

The first step is obvious: If in doing your work the outcome is not good enough, look back at why it didn't work and correct that!

I have a rule of thumb I find encourages me to make the effort to continuously improve: If I do something that seems at all difficult or problematic, I always ask myself, "How could I do this more easily the next time?" and then I act on what I find!

For example, let's suppose I need to reach Matt for a project I'm working on. When I call him I have trouble finding his cell phone number. So, when I find the number, I immediately put it into his contact information. I remember that I need to call Matt again on Friday regarding a document we are working on. If I create a task for this, I can attach the document to be discussed along with his contact information, so when I go to execute the task I don't have to look up this information.

I note on the subject line of the task precisely what I am calling about. When the time comes to act (in this case call), I know exactly what I need to do and I have everything I need to do it with.

Remember, people tend to act when it is easy for them to do so. Make doing the work—the *next time*—easy to do. Many of us are aware of the improvements we need to make, but too often we excuse our lack of action by saying we are too busy to do anything about it. Or we think, "When I have the time I will . . ." The irony is that we do not have the time to *not* act!

By constantly tweaking how we do what we do, we can eliminate waste, remove errors, be a little bit more efficient, and over time, gain more and more control over our work.

## BENCHMARKING

Benchmarking, or the comparing what you do with the best of a class, is a critical tool for improving quality. The comparison tells you how well you're doing and, usually, how to improve. The PEP process first defines excellent personal work systems and organizations and then provides that benchmark for individuals to compare how they process their own work.

You may find some of your team members have developed efficient and effective ways of getting their work done. Use these people as models. They are master performers. If there is a gap between your high and average performers, identify how your high performers execute their work and what behaviors allow them to produce better than your average coworkers.

## FOCUS ON PREVENTION

PEP moves you from a reactive mode to a proactive mode. Putting good planning processes in place enables you to look into the future and prevent problems. It makes you aware of those red flags and indicators that could become fires in the future. Not only are you aware of them, but with a *Do It Now* frame of mind, you act on these things while they're manageable and you can prevent serious problems from occurring.

## PROJECT-BY-PROJECT IMPROVEMENT

Joseph Juran, an American quality consultant who introduced management systems that plan, control, and improve quality, emphasizes the need to improve quality by using project-by-project improvement plans. Dr. Juran stresses that management's role is to provide planning and guidance to improve quality. Translating quality concepts into action at every level is management's job. Management's role is to help improve the skills and knowledge of its staff to plan work and accomplish actions that will improve quality and increase productivity.

## CONTINUOUS CHANGE

People have a very difficult time dealing with change. And yet, continuous improvement is all about continuous change. Top executives can dictate, but most effective managers prefer to involve their people.

Continuous change is hard to deal with if personal goals and desired end results are not clearly stated and regularly reviewed. Project management, time management, work-space organization, follow-up, and follow-through are all components of continuous improvement.

From a PEP perspective, quality improvement has three main ingredients:

1. Identify what needs to be improved.
2. Plan the actions to improve it.
3. Push the plans through.

## SUMMARY

*Lean (manufacturing) is a strategy for remaining competitive through the endless pursuit of waste elimination.*
—DEFINITION, GEMBA RESEARCH

Early in my professional career, I learned there is no lack of demand on you to produce: The sale. The report. The product. The number. And, there is no equal pressure to improve the process involved in the creation of what is demanded.

Lean is itself a process. It is the continuous process of identifying, reducing, and eliminating the waste and obstacles to the smooth flow of production. Lean is a way of thinking. How can I do what I do better—faster—easier—always? Continually searching out improvements.

My friends and business partners Michael and Lynn Valentine have been applying the Lean process principles with the Personal Efficiency Program. They have found that PEP complements and aligns with the philosophy of Lean Thinking. True to Lean philosophy, this represents, "back to basics operational excellence based on what the customer perceives as value."

(For managers, see Chapter 10 for how to accelerate this whole process. For the rest of us, make continuous improvement part of your everyday work!)

## FOLLOW-UP FOR CHAPTER 8

**1.** PEP has the potential to be a critical success factor for you and for your company. PEP addresses how you process your work. It isn't enough to be proficient and technically skilled to do your work; you have to understand the principles of work organization and the application of these principles to your job.

**2.** Make *Kaizen* part of your work process. Seek out ways to improve on your work processes. If a piece of work is at all difficult or problematic, ask yourself the question, "How can I do this more easily the next time?" and act on what you find!

**3.** Apply 6S to your workspace. Eliminate the clutter; have a place to put things, and put things back where they belong; label everything so it is easy and intuitive for you to find things; clean and organize as you work; establish routines to keep it all in perfect order.

**4.** Select a model you can use as a benchmark in improving your efficiency and effectiveness.

# Do It Now!—From Wherever You Are!

## Being Effective in a Mobile Work Environment (MWE)

*The office is where you are—not where it is.*

*Work is something you do—not a place you go to.*

# Chapter 9 Preview

In this chapter you will learn:

- A working definition of the Mobile Work Environment (MWE).
- Major trends of the MWE.
- Issues and solutions on learning to work in the MWE.
- Tips on working effectively in your MWE.

# EVOLVING WORK ENVIRONMENTS

## Why Now?

At least since the 1970s, and probably for many years before, the business world has been seeking sound alternatives to what has evolved into "Dilbert Cubicles." Many of our clients have told us they have known for years that, at any given time, their office space was often thinly occupied by staff and they were paying excessive fixed overhead expenses which depleted bottom-line profits. Clients also told us of their concern that employees often got into ruts, restricting their conversations and brainstorming envelope to a repetitive and limited number of associates.

It now appears, wherever you turn in the working community, that "alternative" offices are being explored, embraced, and adapted. Why now, early in the twenty-first century, is this continuing to happen? One word—*technology.*

Technology has brought us mobile computing, personal information managers, cell phones, pagers, e-mail, vmail, instant messaging, satellite phones, the Internet and organizational intranets and portals, Skype, BlackBerrys, text messaging, scanners, and multifunctional devices. Each of these technologies has contributed to the distillation of the office culture or, as Frank Becker of Cornell University calls it in his benchmark book with Fritz and Steele, *Workplace by Design,* "Workplace Ecology."

Today's mobile communications give us the ability to store and retrieve information (given that we correctly implement and practice effective organizational principles) from wherever we are, whenever we want. High-speed, broadband, and wireless technology has given us access and continual connectivity to whatever we want, from wherever we are. Now, there is an upside and a downside to all this. Just have lunch in most restaurants (some lately have been smart enough to deal with this problem) and you'll hear the "ringing": the downside. Conversely, what great customer service it is to respond to an urgent client call from your car, an airport, or even, if you must, when jogging: the upside. Today, "The office is where you are, not where it is."

The entry of wireless communication into the office allows all-the-time and real-time global access to almost anyone, anywhere. Fast, reliable connectivity to e-mail, vmail, and the corporate server has made it unnecessary for employees to be anchored to a specific geographic location. Factor in the Internet/intranet, coupled with instant messaging, and it becomes even clearer how technological advances have forever changed the needs of the work space of today and tomorrow. We can, because of technology, be wherever we need or want to be and accomplish our work. And again, "The office is where you are, not where it is."

## What Is a "Mobile Work Environment"?

Although change is a constant, the speed of change in the work environment, granted us by technology, has powered-up to today's net-speed 24/7 culture. We think the best lexicon for this new work environment is "Mobile Work Environment" or "MWE."

Organizations have also identified this process by a wide variety of titles—for example, Hewlett-Packard's "Workplace Transformation" project, and Jones Lang LaSalle's "Workplace Strategies (WS)" project. Additional widely used terms include virtual, hoteling, freespace, and mobile office.

I prefer to view these workplace changes as continuous evolutionary steps, and therefore have selected "Mobile Work Environment (MWE)" as the one term that most correctly describes the various paths of change being traveled in the workplace. Regardless of what the MWE is called, there is no doubt it is, and will always remain, a "work in progress." Clearly, five years from now, work processes and tools will be very different than they are today.

## Working Out of a Home Office

Whether working for others or on our own, the closest many of us come to an "office" can be found in our homes. Home office situations can be broadly divided into three basic types:

### Small Home-Based Business (Easiest)
- Few, if any, staff
- All information and decision making take place at one source

### Entrepreneur (More Difficult)
- Consultants, independent sales reps, writers, and so on
- Work with a few people at a time
- Gather information from a wide array of sources
- Used as a base to travel from

**Corporate Employees (Most Difficult)**
- Managers, administrators, staff consultants, sales reps
- Interface with large groups of people
- Large volume of information routinely exchanged with many people
- Many varied sources of information
- Strong need to be connected to others

## COMMON DENOMINATORS

All three types of home offices have two common denominators that must be addressed in order for them to work effectively. They are:

**1.** *Making Choices with Personal Issues.* This is both a blessing and a curse. From a blessing side, you don't need to get dressed, put on makeup or shave, or spend time commuting. No one can see what you look like when you're in your home. Well, not in most cases (the growing use of video will have its own set of issues to be dealt with over the next few years). The core issue for both those who work in a home office environment and those who supervise home office workers is the *result of work,* not hours worked.

Since most of my associates and I are home office workers, I can tell you from firsthand experience that, if anything, most home office workers work *too many hours,* not too few. "Measuring by results," both for the worker and for management, is the only thing that counts. Our somewhat blunt observation is that *managers* fear losing control and *leaders* measure by results.

If a home office worker goes to her daughter's soccer game for an hour or two that's a wonderful quality of life improvement, which can bring high return to any organization. Go to that soccer game! Yet make sure you establish routine working hours so you get out of the office on time. I do so and know that through the consistent application of PEP habits and planning principles discussed in Chapters 2 and 5 of this book, other home office workers can also put in a fully productive, yet reasonable workday.

**2.** *Understanding That Organizational Systems and the Control of Information Are Critical Issues.* If you are a corporate worker with a home office and are some distance away from the corporate facility, you can't afford to not have all the information you need to complete your work. Control and organization of both paper and electronic-based information is critical to the effective accomplishment of your work. Although the ability to move files and documents through the Internet as either links or attachments is routine, it is still not easy to get assistance from others to share information. The reality is that it's likely the people you're looking to for assistance are also working in an MWE and are not easily available at the moment you need them. More than ever, we must take (read as *invest*) the time to plan, prioritize, and anticipate our future work needs.

## The Proper Work Tools for the MWE

Everyone working in the MWE needs to have the proper equipment to be productive and effective. In most situations, the proper equipment means a reasonably current, powerful computer with current versions of the organization's software such as Microsoft Outlook or Lotus Notes, as well as the organization's correct tools for mobile work such as read-write CDs, DVDs, flash memory sticks, scanners, printers, fax machines, cell phones, PIMs, and perhaps an instant messaging system. These types of tools are usually considered "normal fare" in an office. The move to the MWE requires alignment and upgrading of these work tools as necessary to best support your new work mode.

One of the most often heard comments from the people we work with is, "I have to keep this document/information in my paper files because it's not available electronically." We then ask if a scanner is available. Too often, people are not using scanners at anywhere near the capability this tool has to support the MWE. A scanner is the best way to control the volume of paperwork that comes across your desk. With a home office you are unlikely to have enough space for vital things, let alone the never-ending accumulation of paper.

A scanner provides an important component to solving the paper issue. Virtually all information, including old typewritten letters, pictures, magazine articles, and handwritten notes, can be converted into electronic data.

*It is important to remember that with scanned documents, as with all other electronic documents, the core issue still remains how to organize and store information so it can be quickly retrieved when it is needed.*

## Work Issues in the MWE Home Office

An effective home office is one that creates an efficient environment to control, maintain, and retrieve the information used to plan and complete work. The factors that make it effective are:

**1.** *Dedicated Work Space.* This is imperative. The dining room or kitchen table does not work. Within a small apartment, the dedicated space may be a screened-off area of the room. In a modest home or larger apartment, the home office space may be a section of a room. And, of course, in a large home, one room can usually be dedicated as the home office.

**2.** *Furniture Needs to Be of High Quality.* This is not to say that you should spend lots of money. Your options include buying new furniture from a major manufacturer who has designed products for the home office worker. Most corporations have negotiated very attractive, deeply discounted prices with major office furnishing manufacturers. Office furnishing is one of those businesses where 50% or more off the list price means you've got a fair deal.

**3.** *Sound Can Either Distract or Help You Focus.* We all respond differently to sound, and these differences in our human condition must also be considered when making home office decisions. Do you concentrate better with background music? How will you or your clients respond to a dog barking or children playing in the background? Most are very understanding and even a little jealous of your ability to work from home.

**4.** *Planned Work Hours.* The office is where you are. As such, we need to focus and operate in a businesslike manner. I have found it best to establish regular business hours. Everyone in my family knows and respects that during business hours, although I am just in the next room, I am at work and am not to be disturbed unless it's for a very, very good reason.

**5.** *Support Needs—Outsource or Other Options.* When working at home in the MWE, we often need to proactively identify resources that can help us or fix things. I keep a complete "Help and Fix" list in my computer contact list, by categories, with the phone numbers of all the people and organizations I can go to for help or to fix things. I have a computer "guru" who I can call and get advice from, or who will come to my house and fix my computer or adjust my software. I have a printer-repair person who makes house calls in less than two hours.

My contact list has the telephone numbers of help desks, and also includes (when I can get them) the direct dial numbers of people who have helped me in the past, for all my software and electronic tools. If you are a corporate worker, you would also include the specific names and telephone numbers of people at all the various help desks within your organization.

**6.** *Home Alone and Lonely.* One can feel isolated when alone for many hours a day. I make it a point to get out of the home office daily for lunch. Some places (Starbucks, for example) encourage like-minded mobile workers and independents working out of the home to gather. Even though the people have completely different jobs, those who do this say it creates improved social conditions, and participants end up becoming pseudo coworkers, providing helpful feedback and advice—with the added benefit of no office politics!

Additionally, working mostly in an MWE home office may not mean there is no corporate office. If it is geographically logical, plan to spend part of your workweek in the corporate office. Researchers at IBM learned that if teams went three days without gathering, their productivity and happiness suffered. Our advice: Spend at least one day out of every week in the corporate office. We have also heard from our clients that it is best to vary the day of the week you go to the corporate facility.

## Common Issues Faced Working in the MWE

### Using a PIM

We're going to use the term "PIM," which stands for "Personal Information Manager," for the rest of this section, fully understanding that there are several brands of these cell phone/e-mail devices used in the business world, such as BlackBerry and Palm's Treo, as well as others.

PIMs are small, palm-size, handheld electronic devices that can essentially do everything you can do with Microsoft Outlook or Lotus Notes on your regular computing device, as well as those functions done by the typical cell phone.

Please beware that the capabilities of an individual user of a PIM connected directly to a cellular provider has much different and more limited capabilities than a PIM being operated with the technical program capability available from a large organizational entity.

It is important that you understand the capabilities of your PIM before spending time trying to do something you can't do. For example, most organization-supported PIMs allow you to file e-mails directly into a folder system developed by you or the organization on your corporate computer. An individual PIM user, such as myself, does not have this capability. So again, please seek clarity as to what functions your PIM can and cannot support.

Clearly, the current driver for the massive popularity of PIMs is the ability to receive and send e-mails. The "invasiveness" of e-mail has made it necessary for most of us to review how we are using PIMs, especially when it comes to e-mail. (For a full description of good e-mail processes and behavior, see Chapter 6.)

We'd like to offer some rules of the road as far as using PIMs:

**A.** Become an expert on using the keyboard of your device.

**B.** Know and master the word typing option available in your device.

**C.** Familiarize yourself with the quick keys and shortcuts available on your device.

**D.** Set your PIM for automatic synching with your laptop or desktop computer.

**E.** Turn off the alarm/alert function of your PIM so you are *not* notified of every e-mail you receive as you receive it.

**F.** Password protect your PIM in case of loss.

**G.** Identify whether an e-mail you delete on your device will appear on your computer e-mail system.

**H.** Maintain your PIM. Back up the information regularly, periodically empty the cache, speed up processing by deleting the call logs, and so on, to keep your device running properly.

**I.** Send links with e-mails whenever you can. Capacity issues of PIMs make it hard to read long attachments.

**J.** Have an excellent subject line so that people understand what an e-mail is about even before they open it.

**K.** Decide proactively when you will check voice and e-mail on your PIM and stick to it. Don't let e-mails control you.

**L.** When processing e-mail, voice mail, paperwork, and so on, follow the four Ds!

**M.** Get out of the habit of catching up on e-mail and work after work hours. Turn off your cell phone/PIM in the evenings and weekends, and let others know that you do this. Figure out how to get your work done in the scheduled work hours you have planned for it.

## Work Issues in the MWE

**1.** *Client, Hotel, or Airport.* The office is where you are, and work is something you do—no matter where you are in the MWE. I travel the world supporting my various business units and have found that effective planning is my key to having everything I need, regardless of where I am or what I am doing.

Before any travel, appointment, or meeting, schedule a time on your electronic calendar to plan, in detail, where you are going and what you will need to carry out your business purpose successfully. Plan It Now! This will assure you the success you need to win in the business world.

**2.** *Proper Support/Equipment Needs.* Remember the "Help and Fix" contact list I talked about in the section on working at home? I keep this list with me all the time so I can get in touch with my support network if I should need them.

I also find it best to keep a small amount of stationery, company literature, business cards, and postage stamps in my briefcase. You never know when you might want to send a quick, handwritten, thank-you note or brochure to someone you just met or spoke with. In this electronic world we live in, a handwritten thank-you note will make a greater impression than an e-mail saying the same thing.

**3.** *Getting It All Done on Time.* Those of us who are in the MWE still need to schedule time to be either in the corporate office or the home office to do the work that comes from all this traveling. We have learned that *every one-hour meeting typically generates two additional hours of work.* Some of this work is preparation for the meeting, and the remainder is the actions and tasks that result from the meeting. While traveling, I begin to detail my schedule for when I return to my office. "Plan It Now" assures that I keep my promises to my clients and associates.

## FOLLOW-UP FOR CHAPTER 9

**1.** Identify what type of MWE works for you.

**2.** Notebook users may need to establish an effective backup system to assure against the loss of electronic data. Decide, based on your new data activity, how often you must update your notebook, what offline or network storage process you will use, and how often you will back up your data. Backups, if necessary, should be done no less than once a week.

**3.** If you primarily work at home, plan your office hours and advise family members, friends, and associates. Figure out how to get your work done in the allotted hours.

**4.** Your home office requires an environment where your work can be accomplished in an effective manner. If you are home officing, review your current (both physical and human) situation, the shortcomings in this environment, and the steps you need to take to create a value-added environment that assures productivity.

**5.** Familiarize yourself with the quick keys, shortcuts, and functionality of your PIM.

**6.** If you are a mobile worker for a larger company, get into the office at least one day a week.

**7.** If you are a home worker and you are feeling isolated, consider spending some time each week at a local café or restaurant that caters to the mobile worker.

Last, but certainly not least, turn off your cell phone/BlackBerry/PIM on weekends.

# CHAPTER 10

# Be a *Do It Now* Manager!

*If you wait for people to come to you, you'll only get small problems. You must go and find them. The big problems are where people do not realize they have one in the first place.*

—W. EDWARDS DEMING

# Chapter 10 Preview

In this chapter, you will learn how to:

- Successfully get others organized.
- Make the best use of your newfound time.
- Employ one of the most effective means of delegating work.
- Practice effective management with the principle of walkabout.

I once delivered the Personal Efficiency Program (PEP) at a manufacturing plant in England. The participants included managers, administrators, and shop supervisors. I had several PEP coaches with me to facilitate the program; in fact, my participation was limited to introducing the concept and getting a few participants started. One supervisor was particularly enthusiastic about the prospect of getting better organized. He wanted to know all about PEP and how he might use it. I told him, "If you think PEP is good for you, wait until you see what it can do for the people who work with you."

I suggested that the most effective use of his newfound discretionary time would be to move around the shop floor to visit with his people every day and to find out firsthand from them what they needed to get themselves better organized to produce what they needed to produce.

When I returned to the manufacturing plant a few months later, I was approached by the same supervisor. He excitedly described his experience with PEP. He asked if I had known about the strike that occurred in the plant the month before. I told him I had heard about it but didn't know the details. He asked, "Did you know that the whole factory went on strike except for my section?" He said that when senior managers looked into why his was the only section not going on strike, they found that the employees in his section had no complaints. They said that all of the things that they had felt were wrong had been dealt with and handled by the supervisor during the previous months.

The kinds of things this *Do It Now* manager did are described in this chapter.

## MANAGEMENT BY WALKABOUT

One of the most important tools a manager has to get things done effectively and efficiently is a technique called management by walkabout (MBWA), or as some call it, visible management or management by wandering around.

Through the process of MBWA, getting around to my people and seeing what they had to deal with and what problems they faced, I created PEP.

Years ago I worked as a manager in a business where the employees were under tremendous pressure to supply services, produce products, and get them out the door. I was responsible for some two hundred people. A typical day consisted of meeting with the senior management team to discuss internal issues and meeting with customers, then doing lots of paperwork, primarily to satisfy the reporting demands of the higher executive levels. My job was a study in crisis management. I seldom, if ever, was able to leave the office.

But then two things helped me change that. First, I got myself organized. I had help in establishing routines with my assistant, and I began to deal more effectively with the paperwork I was responsible for. Second, I used the time resulting from my reorganization to get out of the office and practice management by walkabout. I spent nearly half the day every day getting out to visit with every single person I was responsible for. I would stop at their desks or work areas, sit down, and chat with them to find out how things were going. I soon realized that most of the people were working extremely hard, but they were not being very efficient or effective in their work. The general scene was one of disorder.

When I first started MBWA, people were suspicious. They wondered why I was there and what I was looking for. But this suspicion quickly went away when they found that I would come back regularly and that I showed a genuine interest in what they were doing. Soon they began to open up and address long-term productivity issues. I listened intently to what they had to say and tried to respond to their expressed needs.

If I didn't respond to a need, I felt very uncomfortable facing the person again. MBWA forced me to be effective in dealing with the issues that were brought up, especially those issues that I wholeheartedly agreed should be dealt with.

I discovered that most of the people I managed had no idea how to work effectively. It wasn't that they didn't work hard; in fact, they obviously worked much harder than they really needed to. That's when I discovered that if I could help them do something to improve how they did their work, I would get the most results from my efforts as a manager.

This was MBWA with a twist. Yes, I listened; yes I watched how the work was being done; yes, I responded, but I also coached them how best to organize themselves and get on top of what they needed to do. I coached them on how to organize and improve their work processes. I helped them improve their organizing skills and apply them to their work environment. This was not just lip service: I visibly coached and facilitated the process. I would not only listen, I would look. After noticing a disorganized condition, I would try to discover the underlying causes. What I often discovered was that people could no longer see their actual working conditions.

For example, I might ask a staff member to clean out his desk. Once he had finished the task, I would look at the desk. And more often than not, I would find that things were overlooked or not even seen by him in the first place.

I have come to believe in black holes, or at least in the black hole phenomena in organizations in which you send something out and it seems to get lost, never to be seen again. Well, those black holes are usually in desk drawers and files. Things simply get shoved away without being dealt with.

Why aren't many important items dealt with? The reasons are many: bad working habits, procrastination, not knowing exactly what to do, poor planning, poor organization, crisis management, and many more. Interestingly enough, rarely do I find that bad intentions or lack of effort are the cause of production difficulties. Often people do not have the authority to handle the problems they face. Or they find things difficult to address, even though another person might find the same things very easy to deal with. Or they feel that every direction they turn, they run into a wall, so they give up trying.

Often I find that arbitrary rules, poor policies, and inefficient work processes create these negative feelings in people. Eliminating these rules and creating new standards almost always improves the morale and productivity of people. What seems like insurmountable and intractable problems to them are, in most cases, within the supervisor's ability to handle. For example, if someone on staff needed a computer to process her work better, I could authorize the purchase immediately, have procurement get it fast, and allow the person to get on with her work with the resource that she needed.

Through MBWA, or what may be described as my PEP Walk, I discovered an extremely effective way to coach people in their jobs. I did this by going through their pending files with them. We would go through each piece of work, one by one, and have them process it then and there. In the pending files, I found procrastination, misunderstanding, and arbitrary rules that prevented people from doing the things they needed to get done. I would have never found these problems simply by asking because, as is often the case, if people had known what the problem was, they would have resolved it. I had to see the process and how they worked to notice that they didn't have the necessary tools, or that they experienced many disruptions, or what was making the work difficult to do.

Within a very short period of time in this management position, I experienced something I had never before experienced—visible results, evident not only to me, but to everybody. The office became much neater. Things were labeled. Common files became comprehensible and usable. People began to take pride in their surroundings. They began to work together to solve the problems that made their work harder to do. The more I concentrated on the basics of work, the more visible the results became.

The more time I spent out of my office on my PEP Walks with the people who did the work—discussing, looking, testing, resolving, eliminating blocks to production, coordinating—the more real production results we achieved and the easier it was to achieve them. This was a complete revelation to me then.

Having since seen how many other companies work, I know that MBWA is not used by executives and managers to the degree it could be. Countless times as a consultant I have been told by people that their boss has never been to their office. Most managers merely pay lip service to the MBWA concept.

I challenge you to use the time you gain through PEP to be out and about with your people and become a *Do It Now* manager. That is PEP's greatest payback. Let us look at why.

## EXAMPLES OF PEP WALK

One of the most effective executives I have ever known ran a bank in Luxembourg. He consistently outperformed his peers, chalking up 20% to 25% return on equity, year after year, in good and bad times.

Neatness and orderliness were his mantras. He had a flat table desk with no drawers in an open office environment. In his view, drawers would only end up keeping the work hidden. He preferred to get the work done and the paper forwarded to where it belonged. He processed his work immediately. He delegated liberally. You would seldom find him at his desk because he spent most of his time around the seven floors of office space. He hated meetings—they were too often a waste of time—so would hold very few of them. Those that he had were held before or after banking hours and were therefore brief and to the point.

He hated clutter and would make this known when he saw it. The bank had a rather large turnover of personnel (being a foreign bank in Luxembourg to which personnel was regularly rotated from the home office for training and experience), so the repeated message for old and new staff was: be orderly; be quick; don't accumulate; get it done, now!

Another example comes from Eunice Johnson, a bank manager who recently had this to say about her PEP Walk experiences:

*I was one of those managers that lived behind my desk until I was introduced to management by walkabout, and I decided to give it a try. The experience was beneficial twofold, as it was enlightening for me and my employees felt a profound sense of appreciation and that their role "mattered" in a very large, diverse organization.*

*From my perspective, sitting with them allowed me to observe the way they did their daily tasks, and it immediately opened my eyes to practices that could have been eliminated, automated, or improved. As I sat and completed the tasks with them, it also gave me a new appreciation for what they did, and I got to experience firsthand how they could easily feel frustrated, depressed, and unimportant. They, on the other hand, were excited and enthused that someone was actually taking the time to show interest in what they did and how they did it. The bonding was great. And, for those moments, I became them, and it meant the world to them that I was making the effort to show interest not only in their work, but in them, as people.*

I can give you many examples of the impact of a PEP Walk. But, better yet—try it! See the next section for tips on how to do it.

## WHY PEP WALK WORKS

Many success factors come as a result of executing PEP Walks. Being out and about, you see and hear things you otherwise wouldn't see and hear. Being out and about prompts you to ask questions and improves your communication and listening skills. Most difficult problems don't go away at the first attempt to deal with them; but, by being out and about with your people, you get their input. You find yourself following up and addressing the problems and testing solutions.

Staff productivity problems are too often affected by things out of their control. To resolve these problems, people who work in other divisions may have to cooperate, even though they have their own priorities. As the manager, you are the only person who can bring these groups together and work out solutions. If you have been out and about, you know the real issues and can help push through solutions.

Another reason why PEP Walk works is simply because people receive much-needed attention. Remember reading about the study done in the late 1930s by a company called Western Electric? They conducted an experiment on improving productivity in the workplace. They found that if they turned the lights up on the factory floor, productivity went up. Then they tested to see what would happen when they turned the lights down on the factory floor. Interestingly, productivity went up again. One conclusion drawn from this study was this: When attention is placed on the needs of people, production increases, even if the things getting attention aren't the right things.

If you are out and about, attending to the issues and needs of the people producing the products, productivity will improve. If in the process of a PEP Walk you concentrate on the right things, your rewards are that much better.

## HAD I KNOWN!

I know it is very difficult to come up with an original idea. Thirty years ago I was amazed to see the results of managing visibly. I had never seen anyone else do it. I had stumbled upon it in my own attempts to manage people. But I soon saw the concept as both widely recognized and applied. My first contact with it was in Tom Peters and Robert Waterman's *In Search of Excellence* (Harper & Row, 1982). They refer to it as "Visible Management." I was delighted to see others found this method of management superior to any other I had witnessed.

My interest in the subject led me to find out that the Japanese, at least in manufacturing, have it down to a science. The Toyota Production System (Lean manufacturing) and Total Quality Management (TQM) are examples.

In Lean speak, it is referred to as the "3 gen" principle: The three principles are (1) where the work is done (gemba), (2) the actual product (thing or service) and the conditions of things in the workplace (gembutsu), and (3) the facts, what is going on, the reality—not what it should be, but what it is (genjitsu). Genchi gembutsu means "go and see for yourself."

*The root cause of any problem is the key to a lasting solution.*
*"Data" is of course important in manufacturing, but I place*
*greatest emphasis on "facts."*
—TAIICHI OHNO

Norman Bodek (author of *Kaikaku: The Power and Magic of Lean*, PCS Press, 2004) calls it *"Gemba Walk."* Gemba Walk, like MBWA and visible management, means going to the place of work and, through observation, questioning, and listening, gathering the facts so remedies can be made. The overriding theme of Gemba Walk is *Kaizen*.

Some subtle differences exist between these "walk to where the work is being done" techniques. MBWA seems to be more about improving relations with the employees. Gemba Walk is both a problem-solving technique and *Kaizen* on the main processes of the concern. It is ironic that there are few examples of their use in white-collar work. In fact, I found when visiting Japan a few years ago, their offices were mostly a mess! No file systems at all were common. Japanese managers would not think twice about visiting the shop floor, but they would be invisible in the back office.

So, more needs to be done to implement this management methodology in the white-collar world. Nevertheless, this method of management works. It gets to the heart of the matter. The best of the best use it. The results will startle you.

## FACE-TO-FACE COMMUNICATION

Our pride often makes it tough to talk about our failings, especially when communicating with our bosses. What might be obvious to others may not be so visible to us. These blind spots create a division or gulf between management and the people doing the work. The best way to bridge the gap is to communicate one-on-one, face-to-face. When you are talking about the same issues on the same level in the same space, you communicate more effectively; PEP Walk creates these golden opportunities to communicate. You encourage open communication when you ask people how they work, what they are doing, and what things will make their lives and jobs easier. PEP Walk means being out there with people, asking questions, and making observations that enable you to comprehend, to listen, to learn.

When I'm out and about in my work, I often ask PEP participants to give me a brief statement of the strategy of their operation. The senior executive of one PEP group was shocked to find that none of the participants in the group, except for himself, could state what the strategy of the operation was. When he and I discussed the matter later, he told me that he thought everyone knew about it. The company had published an annual report about it for all the world to read and in two staff meetings he had covered it in detail.

I didn't find any of this very surprising. In all the years I've been working with companies, only once or twice have I found that employees had any real clue of the strategies being worked on by the company. Too often the companies didn't have a strategy at all. And in companies with a strategy, the communication of it was poor at best.

If you have a message to get across, if you have a plan to get done, if you are trying to execute a strategy, or if you want to explain your vision of the future, there is no more effective method I know than meeting face-to-face with your people.

When on a PEP Walk the manager communicates the vision and strategy of a company continuously through his or her actions as well as words. If the company's strategy is to get the competitive edge through dramatic improvement in the quality of customer service, the manager demonstrates this by actions on the front line with the people who are dealing with the customers and often with the customers themselves. All aspects of communication are greatly enhanced through MBWA.

## FOLLOW-UP METHOD

Chapter 7 discusses the importance of follow-up and follow-through. With PEP Walk, you schedule follow-up and follow-through into your work process. Being out and about with your people is a natural way to follow up and follow through on the things that you want to get done.

## DELEGATION

When I talk with executives about their failures to delegate, the most common reason I hear is how busy their people are and how overwhelmed they would be if they were given any more to do. This perception is often formed by seeing the person's desk piled with papers or by hearing how late he or she stays at the end of the day. A PEP Walk gives you a much more accurate sense of how much work your people do. Moreover, you can see how the work might be spread out differently. My experience suggests that when a manager is out and about, he or she ends up delegating much more and much more effectively.

## WHAT DOES A *DO IT NOW* MANAGER DO?

A *Do It Now* manager provides the resources, encouragement, coaching, and training people need to produce what they need to produce, in as effective and efficient a way as possible. A *Do It Now* manager does this by visibly getting around on the front lines of the business.

## CONCENTRATE ON THE PROCESS OF WORK

To be an effective manager, you should first and foremost focus on the process of the work. In my experience, sufficient pressure is placed on staff to produce, but rarely is sufficient pressure put on *how* the work is produced. If you help people concentrate and focus on the process of work, you will ensure that their job continues to improve and things get easier for them. This focus gets them to resolve core issues and at the same time improves the quality of the product being produced.

Here is what you look for: Are the people well organized? Do they have files that are easy to use, for themselves as well as the people around them? Do they have the tools that they need to produce and are these tools operational? Are they employing good working routines? Do they plan? Do they avoid procrastination?

If beginning MBWA for the first time, focus on the 6Ss.

| | |
|---|---|
| *Seiri* | Organization |
| *Seiton* | Neatness |
| *Seiso* | Cleanliness |
| *Seiketsu* | Standardization |
| *Shitsuke* | Discipline |
| *Sukam* | Habit |

(For an explanation for each S, see Chapter 8, page 168.)

Remember, your most important resource is your people. Most have little idea how their work spaces and work habits impact their effectiveness. Nor typically do they have the skills or training on improving their processes. Most work harder than they need to. By systematically addressing the 6S points at the work space, while the work is being done, asking questions (Why?), observing, listening, identifying abnormalities and deviations from the standard, you can facilitate gradual improvements. By visiting regularly, they know you are serious and committed. By being there and following through, you encourage the discipline and formation of good new habits. Furthermore, you learn a great deal about what works for people and can pass on these learnings to others and speed up the whole process of improvement.

The most effective way to produce change is through small incremental steps. There is no need for the manager to overwhelm his or her personnel with too many things at once. Asking them to deal with and handle one small piece of the puzzle at a time and following up to see that it has been done is all that is usually needed. Again, it is very difficult facing your people once more after you may have promised to resolve some issue and failed to do so. The solution? Deal with it. Handle the issue. And until it is handled continue to keep on visiting the personnel and letting them know what it is that you are trying to do and what you are running into.

After a few months of this, you will find the work spaces of most of the staff will be organized like well-oiled machines. You will have discovered common problems and solved them. Once organized, have your PEP Walks address these common issues. Many of you will have searched out Lean and other TQM tools to further your continuous improvement initiatives. Use Lean and TQM techniques. Remember what brought you there. The *Do It Now* manager makes PEP Walk an everyday activity.

## DON'T BE TIED TO THE DESK

One senior manager, responsible for a division of nine hundred people in a large manufacturing firm, strongly felt that MBWA was one of the most important things he needed to do. But he said that he had no time to do it. He was constantly dragged into other problems, meetings, and crises. He felt tied to his desk.

The solution that he and I worked out was relatively simple. He would spend the whole morning out and about at different sites where his people were located and wouldn't even come to the corporate office until one o'clock in the afternoon. Interestingly enough, with a little bit of organization, screening of information that came to him, improved delegation, and elimination of waste of time, he was able to get out of the office earlier each day, and still put in the extra four or five hours getting around to his people.

Being "tied to the desk" is a common complaint from executives. Simply scheduling MBWA before sitting down at the desk works for some. A more permanent solution is to get rid of the desk completely. One manager did so and operated his business with a clipboard. Not having a desk forced him to get out and about with his people nearly full time. When he had an important meeting, he would hold it in the office conference room.

In his book *Thriving on Chaos* (Alfred A. Knopf, 1987), Tom Peters tells a story of another manager who got rid of his desk and used "a small work area in two departments: a round table with three chairs and a file cabinet in an open area by the entrance door" (p. 428). This allowed him to be accessible and still work with his secretarial support and handle his mail efficiently. I like this idea. If you don't have a desk, you don't have a place to store extra papers and materials that you will never use anyway.

## START WITH YOURSELF

It is human nature to see the cause of one's difficulties "over there." But many improvements can be made within your own area at little or no cost. This experience is common when employing quality improvement processes in companies. If you go after the red herring—a new $9 million computer system when you don't have the money or it will take two years to install it—you will miss the hundreds of improvements you could make in the interim.

## ELECTRONIC TOOLS TO ENHANCE YOUR PEP WALKS

As a manager, you likely have a few layers of management between you and the front lines. Bypassing those can create problems. A solution is to bring them with you, electronically. One way to do your PEP walk is by using electronic tools. If you can't get around often enough to your people, electronic tools can help.

E-mail is one such tool. Inviting employees at all levels to communicate both problems and suggestions directly opens the lines of communication. Your physical presence in their areas periodically makes e-mail that much more effective.

For smaller businesses, networking software allows you to communicate directly through PCs without having to invest lots of money. Lotus Notes, one such software application, is easy to customize for your business. The customized databases can be accessed by anyone authorized in any geographical location with a telephone. Anyone in the organization can participate and contribute to important issues and questions put forward by yourself or others.

With that said, there is no good substitute for physically going to the place where the work is being done.

## MBWA IN AN ALTERNATIVE OFFICE

Management by walkabout assumes management and personnel work in the same location. But as you know, current industry trends are toward getting personnel as close to the customer as possible. For sales and service personnel, that usually means being out of the office in front of customers. Many people work out of the home, at least part of the time. Alternative office designs (open office architecture and facilities where personnel have no permanently assigned space or desks) make it difficult to know where people are at any given time. So what is a *Do It Now* manager to do? Work harder at it! Such work environments make it all the more important to put forth the effort and arrange to visit staff members wherever they may be working.

For many years IBT has provided a special PEP service to company salesforces (and in some cases remote service representatives) where we visit the home offices of remote personnel and help organize their home offices. The most consistent feedback to this very popular program is how valuable it is to have someone from the outside (not outside the company—outside the home) see their work environments. Not only can these outsiders advise on how to set up the office better and introduce routines to make it more pleasant and productive, but also they are in a position of influence so that things that need to be remedied can be remedied quickly and effectively. The function of a PEP consultant is really similar to the role a good MBWA manager can play.

A good manager will arrange to go on sales calls with his or her people and while doing so observe both sales competency and organizational systems to support sales. This might include, for example, how the person has organized his or her car or how easy or difficult it is to connect to the server and process e-mail.

Because so many staffers are now mobile, they are that much further out of the loop when it comes to current strategy or goals (or progress on the strategy or goals). The manager needs to be that much more active relaying news on the company strategies and progress.

Technology such as mobile phones, remote access to e-mail, pagers, and so on all help. Having this technology in place and utilizing it is a first step. But in the case of meetings, there is a qualitative difference between speaking to someone through a telephone conference call and being able to see the eyes of the person sitting across from you as you discuss important issues. And these technology tools are no substitute for your eyeballs when it comes to seeing *how people work as they work,* though desktop videoconferencing may soon make this easier.

Remember, as a manager, your greatest insight will come from where the rubber meets the road.

## SUMMARY

If you are a senior manager, you might think that you have a nearly impossible schedule as it is. Where are you to get additional time in the day to walk about? Sam Walton, the brilliant mind behind the building of Wal-Mart, the largest retail store chain in the world, spent about 80% of his time out and about in his stores. He reportedly traveled four days a week visiting the stores and spent one day in the office. With revenues topping $370 billion, you can be certain Sam could have kept himself occupied in an office. He chose to do otherwise. By being out and about, he solved many management problems directly and greatly reduced paperwork and other time-consuming activities such as devising policy, setting strategy, dealing with the budget, and contacting customers. Sam found that these roles are more effectively carried out with the input of those who have to do the work.

The question then is not how much time you have; rather, it is how you use it. Is it important to you to practice visible management? Is it important to you to know what is going on in the front lines?

The most effective use of management time is getting out and about with people every single day. If you concentrate on the process of work and make it easier for your people to produce, you will do much toward accomplishing the vision, strategy, and goals of the operation.

## FOLLOW-UP FOR CHAPTER 10

**1.** Schedule a block of time in your day to get out and about to your areas of responsibility. The most effective time may be first thing in the morning. If so, don't even bother to come into the office until after you have made the rounds *visibly*.

**2.** Concentrate on the process of work and how it may be improved.

**3.** Communicate the vision. Know the strategy of your operation and communicate that strategy in actions and words. Help your people envision where your operation is going.

**4.** Deliver on what you promise. If you say you are going to do something for an employee, *do it*. If you find it's difficult or impossible, get back to the person and let the employee know where you stand. Do everything in your power to keep your word.

# CHAPTER 11

# Making Meetings Effective

*A meeting is an event where minutes are taken and hours wasted.*

—JAMES T. KIRK

# Chapter 11 Preview

In this chapter you will learn:

- The best meetings might be the ones you do not hold.
- Alternatives to meetings.
- If you must meet to solve a problem, hold it where the problem is.
- If you must meet, do it right!

Our company has been delivering a meeting effectiveness program for many years to great success. One of our European offices was contracted by a large multinational company to devise a scheme to make meetings more effective and productive, with the aim of broadly rolling it out across the world. A number of our people put their heads together with our client to discuss how we might be able to implement such an initiative.

Having devised a scheme, we began our rollout by educating the staff. We immediately ran into a roadblock. When we started our courses, the participants were clear that they were not so much interested in how to make their meetings more efficient and effective as they were in cutting the number of meetings they held. Spending most of their time in meetings, with little time to do the actual work, the staff longed for a solution that would allow them to cut down on the number of meetings they had to attend. This obviously influenced our initiative. Many words of wisdom express the importance of making meetings more effective or efficient, but if you shouldn't have a meeting in the first place, then who cares how well run it is?

I ran into a similar conundrum with a large automotive client. A senior executive asked for my help in figuring out ways to do his job more effectively and efficiently. We performed an analysis of his time and discovered that he had 50 hours of regularly scheduled meetings each week. This left him virtually no time to do any other work. So, the issue wasn't making him more efficient in his meetings, it was how to cut the time he was spending in meetings, leaving him time to do the things he was actually being paid to do.

*Meetings are indispensable when you don't want to do anything.*
**—JOHN KENNETH GALBRAITH**

How bad is the problem? One study found that professionals attend, on average, 61 meetings per month (MCI Conferencing White Paper, "Meetings in America"). In their book, *Better Business Meetings* (Irwin, 1995), Robert B. Nelson and Peter Economy found that over 50 percent of meeting time is wasted.

How can highly educated and competent professionals fall into the trap of wasting 50 percent of their meeting time? This is not only an issue of running well-planned and efficient meetings. Most meetings should simply not be held. Meetings are inefficient because the solution to the issues being addressed can never be found in a meeting. Most meeting topics can only be properly addressed at the point where the work is being done.

I should mention I am not trying to examine all aspects of effective meetings in this chapter, but rather key points that apply, support, and reinforce the PEP philosophy. So "screening unnecessary information" applies by "not holding unnecessary meetings" as well as by "not bringing back handouts to your office that you can access electronically." *Do It Now* applies to sending out the agenda, reading the briefing materials, starting on time, circulating minutes promptly (or better yet *in* the meeting) and so on; *Plan It Now* applies to always making clear the action items and who is responsible before adjourning, and so on. Many fine books cover this topic in a much more thorough way. However, I believe you will find some of these PEP learnings to be of use.

In this chapter, I cover two basic topics: how to avoid meetings in the first place and how to run a meeting well.

> *Meetings are a symptom of bad organization. The fewer meetings the better.*
> —**PETER F. DRUCKER,** *The Effective Executive*
> **(Harper & Row, 1966)**

Meetings have evolved into the preferred method of managing by professionals. The problem is that meetings are typically not the forum to solve problems and come to correct decisions. Yet the vast majority of professionals spend the bulk of their time in meetings. Why are meetings such a waste of time? If they are run poorly, not much is accomplished. Educating people in how to run a proper meeting doesn't necessarily result in a positive outcome, either.

One reason meetings are so often ineffective, even when they are well run, is due to the distance between those in the meeting and the place where the work is actually being done. If you want to effectively deal with a problem, you need to experience the situation firsthand. Too often, issues come up in meetings by way of e-mail, phone calls, or other alerts. Then, a meeting is held from a remote location and a solution is created based on limited information, leaving participants to depend on the information forwarded from the location where the work is taking place. That information is often simplified and abstracted from its context when reported (mostly to summarize and keep the meeting from going too long). As a result, the meeting participants don't have the facts, but a filtered version of some of the facts. Any conclusion they come to will not be based on an accurate reflection of the actual situation.

**Figure 11.1** Hold problem solving meetings where the work is being done.

If you are holding a meeting to solve a problem, forget it. Instead, go to the place where the problem exists, observe, ask questions, and see the work being done. Soon you will begin to discover the real situation. (More on this later in the chapter.)

## PART ONE: CUTTING DOWN ON THE NUMBER OF MEETINGS

### Meeting Analysis

To cut down on meetings, begin by reviewing the meetings you have attended recently to evaluate their relevancy, importance, and purpose. Go through your calendar for the past couple of months and, with a critical eye, examine each of the meetings you attended.

Calculate the average number of hours per day you spent attending meetings. Ask yourself:

- What was the purpose of this meeting?
- Could the purpose have been accomplished in another way?
- Which of these meetings could be considered "routine"?
- Are the routine meetings really needed?
- If it was a problem-solving meeting, was the problem solved?
- What alternatives could have been employed instead of a meeting? Phone call? Conference call? Video conference?

*Any simple problem can be made unsolvable if enough meetings are held to discuss it.*

—UNKNOWN

Meeting techniques don't matter if you're not going to hold a meeting. As with e-mail, cutting down on the volume of meetings can be a complex and difficult thing to do. Corporate culture often dictates that meetings be held. Nevertheless, with so many people complaining that meetings are a waste of time, leaving them no time to do their actual work, it seems only reasonable that we take great effort to cut down on the number of meetings people attend.

---

*Tip:* One pharmaceutical executive managed to cut down on meetings simply by blocking out time in her calendar for work. When someone wanted to have a meeting with her, they would have to find an open time in her calendar. Since her calendar had time blocked out for important work, it limited the number of hours available for meetings.

---

- Evaluate the need for a meeting in the first place
- Explore alternatives to meetings.
- If there's a problem, forget about having a meeting, and go to where the problem is.

## Go. See. Confirm.

The only way to truly comprehend the nature of a problem is to go to the workplace, observe the actual conditions, and collect the facts.

This leads to a greater understanding of reality. Otherwise, any solutions we invent in the meeting room are for problems that are not really happening in the workplace. This is the reason problem solving begins with the saying, "Go and see for yourself, in the workplace, where the work is actually happening" (Brian Lund, *Go See Confirm,* Genchi-Genbutsu). This process is employed by Toyota's supervisors, managers, and others accountable for solving problems in the business. Toyota's president, Katsuaki Watanabe, describes the process as follows:

- Go to the place.
- Do firsthand observation.
- Talk to the people involved.
- Gather the facts.
- Define the problem based on the facts.

Watanabe says that problem solving needs to be done in the actual place where the work is being conducted, instead of in meetings or conference rooms. Much of the technique, along with the steps and information needed to understand the concept of the "PEP Walk" is covered in Chapter 10. If problem solving is conducted according to these steps, both the need for and the number of meetings will diminish.

If you must hold a meeting, consider holding it in the location where the work is being done. Meeting participants can observe with their own eyeballs and listen with their own ears to the issues defining the problem. You will discover that by instituting meetings at the location, your meetings will probably be shorter, more effective, and your decisions will certainly be more realistic.

I cannot leave this section without mentioning, once again, that since most supervisors and managers have white-collar or administrative support, having supervisors apply the principles of the PEP Walk will also produce the best results for them because it gets the staff to focus on the 6S principles. (See Chapter 10: "Be a *Do It Now* Manager!" for more detailed steps for applying the 6S principles.)

Although this approach to problem solving will not eliminate the need for all meetings, it can certainly be employed in circumstances where problems exist, and the real solution won't be an abstract discussion around a conference table, but going to where the problem is, identifying the facts, and working out a solution from there.

# PART TWO: IF YOU'RE GOING TO CALL A MEETING, RUN IT RIGHT

You have now analyzed the meetings you've attended in the recent past and discovered ways to eliminate some of them. You have embraced the concept of going to the source of the problem and then observing, listening, gathering facts, and coming up with solutions. As a result, you have fewer meetings to attend. Even so, there will always be other meetings you must attend.

Let's begin by identifying the different types of meetings. The type of meeting influences the composition of attendees and the preparation required.

- *Briefing Meetings*. These are generally held as information-sharing activities and are typically held regularly. It might be a department manager getting everyone together on a Monday morning to brief everyone on the activities of the previous week, share plans, and remind people of activities during the upcoming week. It might be a company-wide presentation by the president. There are really no limits to the number of people who may attend a briefing meeting. Preparation is usually limited to just the speaker.
- *Planning Meetings*. Executives may need to discuss the strategic aims and initiatives for an upcoming year or quarter, or incorporate a budget planning process into their strategic plan. Planning meetings may be held among project team members both to figure out the next steps to be taken as well as to monitor progress on a project.
- *Recurring Meetings*. Regular meetings between a project manager and his or her direct reports (one-on-one) would be examples of recurring meetings. Project teams may set up recurring meetings to monitor progress of a project. Recurring, scheduled meetings are the first place to look when cutting down on meetings. Often, routine meetings are so routine we never question why we are having them in the first place.
- *Problem-Solving Meetings*. These could also be referred to as topical meetings. They have a specific subject and arise as a result of some situation that has occurred. As discussed earlier in this chapter, many of these meetings can be eliminated or avoided by replacing them with a PEP Walk. Going to the source of the problem, observing and gathering facts, and having discussions with people on the scene often help those accountable to accurately

identify the problem and come up with solutions that can be applied then and there. If a meeting is necessary to solve a problem, it should be held at the point where the work is being done.

- *Debriefing Meetings*. What the military calls "after action reviews" are held to determine what lessons were learned: What was done well that we want to repeat? What could we have done better that we want to remember in future similar situations?
- *Decision-Making Meetings*. These meetings might be held at the board or senior executive level. In a financial institution, they might include a credit committee meeting to approve credit transactions, or in the case of a board, they might include executive decisions such as hiring, firing, and salaries.

---

***Tip:*** In *Science Lessons: What the Business of Biotech Taught Me about Management* (Harvard Business Press, 2008), Gordon Binder, former CEO of Amgen, demanded that every major decision be made in the course of one meeting. Any and all interested parties were encouraged to attend and participate. He found it made everyone feel included and cut down on the number of meetings. 'When you make it clear that you're hell-bent on making a decision . . . people focus."

---

- *Reporting and Presenting Meetings*. These are designed to deliver a report or a presentation to higher-level bodies within the organization.

"The three evils of meetings:

**1.** Meet but don't discuss.
**2.** Discuss but don't decide.
**3.** Decide but don't do.

—**TAKESHI KAWABE**"

## Well-Run Meetings

If you have been diligent in analyzing your existing meeting schedule, eliminating those meetings you do not need, using a PEP Walk to solve problems, and have now cut down on the number of meetings you attend, the next step is to learn how to run a meeting properly when you need to.

For meetings to run efficiently and productively, they must be properly prepared for:

- Determine if you need a meeting in the first place. Could the matter be resolved over a short telephone call or a clear and simple e-mail? If you have determined that a meeting is the best way to resolve the issue, then:
- Identify the exact purpose and objectives for the meeting. Develop a clear picture of what you intend to accomplish in the meeting, including any expected decisions to be made, and issues to be resolved.
- Determine who should attend the meeting in order to accomplish your intended outcome. How many people will be involved in the meeting? (*Note:* Decision-making meetings should have a limited number of people in attendance. Typically, anything over six or seven people in attendance makes decision making unwieldy. If it's a briefing meeting of some sort, there aren't necessarily any limitations on the number of people who should attend.)
- Determine a time, a place, and an expected duration for the meeting.
- Prepare an agenda for the meeting in advance.
- Send out any relevant briefing materials to the meeting participants in advance, so they can familiarize themselves with the materials before the meeting is held.
- Define the roles of the personnel in the meeting. (Is it necessary to have someone facilitate the meeting? If meeting attendees tend to get testy or in some ways make it difficult to reach a good outcome, consider a facilitator to keep the meeting on track. Also, consider assigning someone to take notes and someone to manage the time. A note taker would compile notes of the meeting and put together a summary of the minutes at the end, while a timekeeper would enforce the meeting's schedule.)
- If decisions are required, identify the decision-making procedure. Some useful options include: democracy (majority rules), unanimous (everyone must agree), or the team proposes and the boss makes the call.
- If it's a particularly important meeting, the chairman may consider visiting with participants in advance. The chairman can better organize the meeting's content, intended purpose, and outcome, so

that the end result is less discussion in the meeting itself, with more decisions being made.

## During Meetings

- Start the meeting on time regardless of who might be missing.
- Clear the purpose and objectives of the meeting with the participants so all agree on the expected outcome.
- Agree on a decision-making process. Will it be true consensus (everyone gets his say and all come to a unanimous agreement)? Will it be true democracy (where majority rules on the decision)? Or will it possibly be a one-person decision—made by the boss—based on the meeting's results and the proposals submitted by the team?
- Keep the meeting on schedule. Note progress regularly. The time-keeper should ensure the meeting ends on time. To keep meetings short, consider holding meetings during lunch, or as one of our offices in Europe does, before the office opens or after the close of business. Or you could hold "stand-up" meetings, in which chairs are not allowed. (Let fatigue limit the length of the meeting.)

**Figure 11.2**  Keep to the meeting schedule.

- Meetings typically take all the time they are scheduled for. Consider scheduling meetings in blocks of 20 minutes or 50 minutes duration. At Toyota, one branch demands that all of its meetings be no longer than 50 minutes, and they must always leave 10 minutes for people to get to the next meeting. At one large pharmaceutical company which held full-day meetings off site, one manager insisted that blocks of time be set aside in the schedule to allow people to handle their e-mail, voice mail, and other things that may come up. By scheduling meetings tightly and enforcing start and end times, meetings can be more efficient.
- Hold your meetings "topless"—meaning, ban any use of laptops, BlackBerrys, cell phones, or any other digital tools during the meeting.
- Use technology to make meetings more effective. The use of a light board and LCD display helps people who prefer to see things visually.

---

*Tip:* One way to cut down on travel time to meetings is to use technology such as videoconferencing or conference calls.

---

- If meeting participants exceed six or seven, and decisions are expected to be made in the group, break the team into smaller groups and allow each group to tackle different aspects of the issues being decided on.
- If a meeting calls for generating creative ideas, consider using the brainstorming technique. Brainstorming best works by focusing on an identified issue and encouraging participants to come up with as many solutions, proposals, and ideas as possible, and then pushing those ideas as far as possible. Write all ideas down. Do not interrupt, criticize, or evaluate suggestions until everyone has had their say and you are ready to evaluate the list of ideas and determine the next steps to take.
- Be decisive. Meetings should result in decisions being made and action points assigned.
- When it comes to the meeting's scheduled ending time, the chairman should summarize the results of the meeting. In this summary, list all of the decisions made.
- At the end of the meeting, "next steps" should be identified and listed. Apply who, what, when, and where to each task. (*Caution:* Too often, the *what* is left a bit unclear, and the *when* can sometimes be totally lost. Make sure they are included.)

- Wrap up the meeting with an agreement on how these steps will be monitored.

## After the Meeting

- All minutes should be compiled the same day of the meeting, including all action steps to be taken. The minutes should be made available to all participants.
- Decide how the minutes will be distributed. Will it be by e-mail? Or is it possible to post the minutes and action steps on an intranet that can be accessed by the meeting participants, with progress tracked there? Remember, the less e-mail the better!
- Aggressively follow through on the action points from the meeting, so they in fact get done.

## SUMMARY

The most effective way to make meetings efficient is to not have them when you don't need to. Make every effort to eliminate nonproductive, ineffective, or unnecessary meetings from your schedule.

If the meeting topic is the resolution of a problem, first apply the PEP Walk, and go to where the problem is, before holding a meeting. If you are convinced you must hold a meeting to solve a problem, hold it at the place where the work is being done.

If you do hold a meeting, prepare, conduct, decide, make a plan, assign the tasks, and follow through on the decisions of the meeting properly.

## FOLLOW-UP FOR CHAPTER 11

**1.** The best meetings may be the ones that are never held. Often, recurring meetings stray from their purpose and need. Begin by analyzing the meetings you've attended over the past couple of months. With a critical eye, evaluate their relevance, importance, and purpose. Eliminate as many as you can.

**2.** When faced with a problem, go to where the problem is taking place and look, listen, gather the facts, and determine if a solution can be directly applied.

**3.** If you must hold a problem-solving meeting, hold it at the place where the work is being done and where the problem exists.

**4.** When calling for a meeting, prepare. Include in your preparation your intended purpose, objectives, agenda, roles, room, time, duration, materials.

**5.** Run meetings well. Start and end on time. Facilitate the discussions to keep the meeting on track. Meet objectives. Make decisions. Note action points (next steps), who, what, when! Distribute minutes.

**6.** Have a follow-up procedure in place. Follow through on tasks so they get done!

# CHAPTER 12

# Maintain It Now

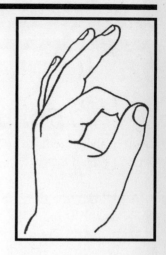

*The time to repair the roof is when the sun is shining.*

—JOHN F. KENNEDY

# Chapter 12 Preview

In this chapter, you will learn:

- A task is done when you have put everything back in better condition than when you picked it up.
- The less you keep, the less you have to maintain.
- The purpose of good maintenance is to make it easy to produce next time.
- You should add tasks to each weekly plan that will create improvements in your work situation.

An associate once told me of a young man whose parents gave him a new car when he turned 18 to celebrate both his high school graduation and his first real job. Although the young man made a point of having his car washed once a week, he never changed the oil in the car. Naturally, when this simple, routine maintenance step was skipped repeatedly, the car's engine parts began to grate and grind against one another. Eventually, the entire engine locked up. The result was a burned-out engine and a useless car, all because ordinary maintenance hadn't been done.

Beyond the loss in monetary terms, what struck me was the foolishness involved and the fact that it needn't have happened at all. Here was a fellow who had neglected the most basic and practical of car maintenance procedures, ignoring routines that should have guaranteed a smoothly operating car for years to come.

As I mulled over this story, I thought, perhaps the parents never taught their son the importance of changing the car's oil. My hunch, though, is that they simply *assumed* that he knew how important it was and that he was changing the oil regularly. It's such a basic, integral part of car maintenance, it may not have crossed their minds that he might not be changing the oil.

People have a very low awareness of maintenance in their administrative work. Executives, when cornered to explain their lack of action on the subject, say they "expect" their people to know these things because "they're professionals." If they think about it at all, they assume someone else is working on it, so they do not demand it be done.

We know the consequence for that young man. The consequence for you of not getting and keeping yourself and your people organized is far more severe than a locked-up engine.

## ENTROPY

Entropy can be defined as a measure or degree of disorder toward the breakdown of any system. In physics, this is the second law of thermodynamics. It is a natural law of the universe that systems will tend to evolve from order to disorder and with this disorder there is increased complexity. Want a simple life? Make orderliness part of your everyday work process!

If you hope and expect to work in an orderly environment, you must recognize the natural tendency for the environment to move in the direction of disorder and *you must work to maintain that order*.

Try neglecting your garden for a while and you will soon see the effect of entropy.

> *Do you ever wonder why things always get cluttered again after you've cleaned and organized? It's a law of the universe, and you can't break it. If you do nothing, you've already lost. Clutter prevails. You can't win against entropy. You can only fight it. You can't even break even. Entropy will always increase. You need to keep adding energy into the system (organizing). The flow of energy maintains order. By adding energy into a system you create organization.*
> —JON MILLER, "5S Your Desk: And Other Tips for Office Productivity," March 21, 2006

You will have hopefully made many changes by now as a result of the book and Personal Efficiency Program (PEP) processes. Maybe your desk is cleaner, your files are organized a bit better, and things are where they are supposed to be. You have a better system in place. You can be assured, because of the law of entropy, any system you have put in place will tend to break down unless you consistently work toward orderly maintenance of the system.

So, what is the trick? Make maintenance part of your work cycle.

## MAINTENANCE AND THE WORK CYCLE

I learned a lesson about maintenance from an old-timer who worked for IBM. He would travel to customer sites and repair their mainframe computers. He would often have younger technicians with him on these jobs. He was the butt of jokes because he had "peculiar" clothes and work habits. He used to wear overalls with dozens of pockets in them. In his pockets were all the different tools he needed or might need. If he saw something to be repaired, even if it hadn't been part of the original repair order, he'd repair it. If he saw a drop of oil on the ground he took out his cloth and cleaned it up, then and there. As he used a tool he cleaned it and put it back in the appropriate pocket. If a tool broke, he had a requisition form in his pocket that he filled out right then to replace the tool. His colleagues would attack the job not bothering to clean up as they went and inevitably when the end of the day came the old-timer was done and ready to go before the others. This was his way of working. He maintained an organized state.

Simply stated, maintenance is part of the work cycle. Think of it this way: Each piece of work, each task, has a beginning, middle, and end. Part of the task beginning must include organizing (planning, preparing, setting up) for the task. In the middle is the act of doing the task. Finally, along with task completion, the ending must include maintenance points, including "put things back where they belong," and "improve the condition of everything you touch" (including files, tools, and so forth).

Maintenance routines should be thought of in the same way. The easiest way to do this is to incorporate basic maintenance routines into your work cycles, in exactly the same planned way you change the oil in your car. In the same automatic way you slide in behind the wheel, insert the car key, and start the engine, you know that the car's oil must be changed on a routine basis if your car is to be in top shape. Why should you expect work to be any different?

For example, how might you handle the job of answering a letter from a regular client? You should start with the client's file, so you have the client's past history of association with your company at hand. You can then refer quickly, easily, and accurately to any pertinent facts. You can verify the spelling of names based on materials sent to you from the original sources. You should be able to cite dates, based on copies of invoices or order forms. You would have copies of all earlier letters to refer to. You'll likely discover resources you didn't know existed.

The point is, by going to the client's file, you don't risk embarrassing yourself (and your company) by being uninformed. What you know influences what goes into the letter, and the quality and content of the letter is likely to be greatly improved.

Assuming you're using a paperwork process, when you complete a letter and get ready to put it into your outbox, what do you do with the client's file? You take one or two minutes to put it in order. Sort letters into chronological order, with the most current letter on top. Eliminate duplicate letters. If there are loose business cards in the file, staple them to the folder itself so they don't fall out of the file and become lost. Or file them in the Rolodex. Two minutes, tops! And when you put the file back, it will be in better shape and more current than it was when you picked it up. That's maintenance.

This maintenance routine applies to your computer files as well. If the composed letter is in the client's directory, quickly glance through the rest of the directory, purge any unneeded documents and organize what's left. A colleague of mine found 1,800 messages in someone's groupware database. No one can use that much information or keep up with it. His client simply didn't organize (or more likely, didn't delete) as he went along. Time is not the issue. The issue is making organization part of the work process.

## MAKE IT EASY

The purpose of maintenance is to make it easy for people to produce. If the copy machine runs out of paper while you're making copies, fill the machine to a functional level. Don't put a dozen sheets in the tray so you can finish your job and leave the next person to run out of paper. Don't leave your files in such a hopeless state that no one, yourself included, can hope to make sense of them. Instead, turn everything you touch into a tool for increased efficiency and productivity.

Your motto should be *"Do things and organize as you do them!"*

Maintenance means organizing yourself in a way that makes forward movement easy. If you empty your stapler, refill it. If you reach in your drawer and you're out of staples, go to supply now and get a box of staples. Fill your stapler and get on with your work. Don't leave small details hanging unsettled, so they trip you up at a later time. Few things are as frustrating when trying to take a telephone message as reaching for a pen and not finding one or going through half a dozen before you find one that actually works. If a pen is out of ink, throw it away; today most pens are meant to be disposable.

## SHOULD YOU BE MAINTAINING IT IN THE FIRST PLACE?

For maintenance to continue, it has to consume as little of your time and effort as possible. Otherwise, being human, you're going to find yourself putting it off "until it's more convenient," or you're "not quite so tired," or "when you have the time" or whatever excuse you may find not to do it. Therefore, you want maintenance to be both efficient and painless.

If you've been thorough in purging your files, you'll have little (or at the least much less) to maintain. If you discover that you are spending time maintaining something you seldom if ever use, you have to question its worth to you. Start questioning why you're maintaining it. If it's something you can honestly do without, do without!

## PREVENTIVE MAINTENANCE

A term used in Lean and quality programs is "Preventive Maintenance." Preventive maintenance can be defined as actions done on a prescheduled or monitored basis to prevent future breakdowns. There are many opportunities to apply this concept to an office environment.

Inventory your office equipment. Find out from the equipment manuals about the expected maintenance routines and schedule them into your calendar.

Nothing can be as frustrating as your computer failing and not being able to access your computer files. The solution is to back up your hard drive. Although it may take a little time, money, and effort to get the backup equipment and software, it is well worth it. Get a backup hard drive, install the software, and set up automatically scheduled backups daily or weekly, and you may avoid a disaster.

Computer maintenance includes cleaning up your Internet files. As you access the Internet, temporary files are created that can slow down your computer. With Windows operating system, periodically open the Internet, go to Tools, Internet Options, General tab, and Browsing History, and you can delete the files and cookies stored on your computer that may slow down its operation.

When you are surfing the Internet, spyware can find its way into your computer that common antivirus applications do not cover. Spyware can silently track your surfing behavior to create a marketing profile of you, which is then sold to advertising companies. Several free software applications (Spyware.com and Ad-Aware at lavasoft.com) can scan your computer for evidence of data mining, aggressive advertising, and tracking components installed on your computer unbeknownst to you. By installing and regularly running these applications on a scheduled basis you will keep your computer free of these unwanted visitors.

Identify what needs preventative maintenance and schedule it into your calendar.

## MAINTENANCE AND *DO IT NOW*

If you have taken to heart the concept of *Do It Now* you will have ample opportunity to reinforce it with maintenance. Why? Because maintenance isn't always the most "important" or most "urgent" thing to do. There will always be reasons to postpone a maintenance action. But if the words *Do It Now* pop into your head when you first recognize some maintenance action, you will act. If you see some tool that needs repair, you will *Do It Now*. If a supply runs out, you will fill it immediately. *Do It Now* becomes the habit and extends itself to maintenance.

## MAKE MAINTENANCE A HABIT

Just as you automatically brush and floss your teeth in the morning, it's best and easiest to establish nonthinking, efficient maintenance routines in your work. As covered in Chapter 4, batching and scheduling the processing of your paperwork and e-mail daily keeps your day-to-day work flow under control. A weekly organizing time can be incorporated into your weekly planning process to maintain your organized state. Bring your filing up to date. Back up your hard drive. Check on your supplies.

Just as you've scheduled a time each day to empty your in basket, you should schedule a time for the big jobs that are so tempting to put off, such as purging your files of any unnecessary clutter they may have accumulated. I have often found people do this sort of complete cleaning of the office at the end of the year, usually between Christmas and New Year's when it seems everything slows down in the office. They use the time to get rid of the old year's papers, set up the next year's files, purge what they haven't used lately, get rid of the stacks of magazines they saved to read, and generally clean up. While this is better than not doing it at all, it is, in my experience, not enough. Purging and cleaning on a quarterly basis seems to work best. Schedule it in your calendar, say half a day. Close the door and get to work reorganizing, purging, going through all of your books, reference files, archives, and such. Figure 12.1 shows a schedule for maintaining your system.

## THE 21-DAY CHALLENGE

An IBT Australian colleague, Sharon McGann, has enjoyed a great deal of success with her students applying what she has dubbed her 21-Day Challenge. At the very beginning of the PEP process, Sharon asks each of her students to select one habit to work on and change for the better. The challenge is to work on the habit every day for 21 days. The catch is if you miss a day, then you go back to the beginning; you must keep at it for 21 consecutive days!

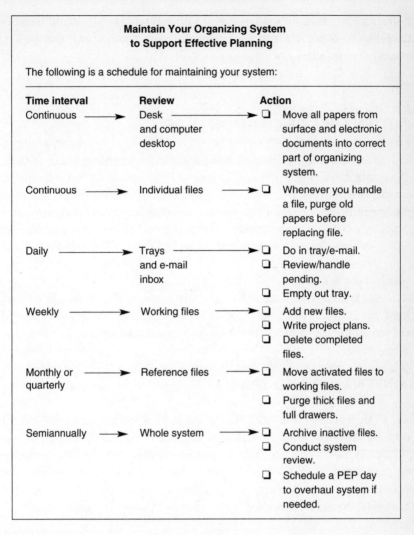

**Maintain Your Organizing System
to Support Effective Planning**

The following is a schedule for maintaining your system:

| Time interval | Review | Action |
|---|---|---|
| Continuous | Desk and computer desktop | ❏ Move all papers from surface and electronic documents into correct part of organizing system. |
| Continuous | Individual files | ❏ Whenever you handle a file, purge old papers before replacing file. |
| Daily | Trays and e-mail inbox | ❏ Do in tray/e-mail.<br>❏ Review/handle pending.<br>❏ Empty out tray. |
| Weekly | Working files | ❏ Add new files.<br>❏ Write project plans.<br>❏ Delete completed files. |
| Monthly or quarterly | Reference files | ❏ Move activated files to working files.<br>❏ Purge thick files and full drawers. |
| Semiannually | Whole system | ❏ Archive inactive files.<br>❏ Conduct system review.<br>❏ Schedule a PEP day to overhaul system if needed. |

**Figure 12.1** Schedule for maintaining your organizing systems.

Progress is monitored and discussed by Sharon and her student throughout the whole PEP process (which might last several months). This habit-changing process becomes the student's personal model of what occurs while trying to develop one new habit. This understanding is then used as a basis for further action plans and other habit changes.

Are you up to the challenge? What work habit would you most like to change? Devise a strategy to change the habit, to substitute a new habit for this unwanted one. And every day for 21 days straight, carry out your habit-changing plan. If you fail one day, begin again from day one. Keep track of your experiences and feelings during this process. Understanding better how you respond to this challenge will make the next challenge that much easier to meet.

## MAINTENANCE OF COMMON FILES

One hard-won lesson learned helping clients maintain their common file organization is if everyone is responsible for the files, no one will take responsibility.

As a team leader, it is up to you to assign *named individuals* responsibility for the department common files. The responsibilities can be divided up—one person for the shared drive files, another for the shared paper files, and so forth. All team members know who is responsible for what.

The same can be said for other common tools. If a common calendar is kept to track team schedules or where people are, it is important that one person be made responsible for its maintenance.

## MAINTENANCE AND TRAVEL

Many of us travel in our work. In my case, I am often out of the country, sometimes for weeks at a time. It is very easy for all of the good work you have done in getting caught up and organized to fall apart because you have been on the road. Furthermore, the traveling itself takes up a lot of time.

Consider these two issues:

1. Making your travel effective and efficient
2. Keeping up with what accumulates while you are away

1. *Making Your Travel Effective and Efficient.* First off, I believe travel is critical to effective management. If the work is being done at a distance, a good manager must go there. (Gemba.)

If you travel simply to hold meetings, you might ask the question: What are the meetings for? Since I believe most traditional meetings are worse than a waste of time, I would seriously question whether what you hope to achieve in such meetings could not be better served by a telephone call or videoconference.

If the purpose of your travel is to meet customers, then you want to organize the travel to get the most out of the visit and do the least harm to the office organization you leave behind.

- If you can, travel by train. Take your laptop with you and work while traveling.
- Batch your travel days so all the necessary traveling is done only on certain days in the week.
- Batch your appointments by location, allowing you to get more done in less time.

2. *Keeping Up with What Accumulates While You Are Away.* Technology enables you to do practically anything on the road that you would typically do in the office. With either a laptop or some Smartphones, you can access e-mail, surf the Web, access and edit documents, and more or less do your job from wherever you are.

Of course there may be complications. When traveling overseas, you may find that your Smartphone doesn't work in some countries. Some companies may have policies or technical issues that prevent you from logging on to the company server. But, in many cases, these issues have been resolved and connecting can still be possible. The trick is to make it a point to access your server and process the bulk of what you get daily and not leave it to be done when you return.

If you have adopted the habit of emptying your e-mail inbox daily, carve out some time while you're on the road to maintain that practice. One client who was consistently keeping up at the office found that when she traveled to meetings, the meeting schedules often consumed every minute of the day. She insisted that time be set aside during the day for a break from the meetings to quickly process her e-mail. Of course, the thinking goes, when on the road you want to get the business out of the way as quickly as possible. But all-day meetings are typically a struggle. Two or three half-hour breaks would not be unreasonable (and will often be energizing). Use these breaks to check in and process (meaning, actually responding to, forwarding to the right person, tasking, scheduling, and filing or deleting) each e-mail and voice mail immediately.

Make it a practice to call the office daily and process whatever has come in. If you have a secretary, establish a routine time to call so that he or she is prepared, and you can quickly go through all that has happened and keep the ball rolling in the office.

Keep up with travel expenses and receipts daily so they do not accumulate.

If actions result from your travel, post them in your to-do lists immediately, noting the specific next steps, due dates, and so on.

Never schedule a meeting for exactly when you return from a trip. Allow yourself a few open hours upon return to wrap up everything from the trip (summary of activities, final receipts, offers/proposals, etc.) and get completely caught up on anything else that may have accumulated while you were away that you were unable to finish or process during the trip.

Over time, you will discover that you become more efficient and decisive in processing your work this way while on the road. Try it.

## MAINTENANCE AND CONTINUOUS IMPROVEMENT

Even after all the times I used the word "maintenance" in this chapter, it is not precisely what you should be concentrating on. Yes, an end product is to prevent you from backsliding into old, nonproductive habits. It isn't enough, however, to PEP yourself up and then concentrate only on keeping things that way. You also have to work to make things better. You should work conscientiously and deliberately to improve how you do your work. In today's fast-paced, competitive environment, it isn't enough to do better and stay that way. You must continue to excel. Even if you've made considerable progress, your real goal should be continuous improvement in everything you do.

I've mentioned that people seldom include tasks on their to-do lists that are geared toward improving how they complete their work. It isn't that people aren't thinking about these things. In fact, with quality and drives under way in most companies, many people are thinking about exactly these things, just not in relation to their day-to-day work. Instead, they think of continuous improvement in terms of maintaining the plant's no-defects product record for a year.

Every week I make it a point to ask myself the question, "What will I do in the next week to improve my work situation?" There have to be several tasks on my weekly plan that will make my work life easier, make me more effective, increase my knowledge, or in some way improve the way I'm doing something.

I might add a task to read two chapters from a software application I'm interested in expanding my use of. I have seen people choose tasks from their personal improvement goals and schedule them into their work calendars. I encourage people to add those spontaneous ideas that come up and act on them. "Learn how to use that new printer" might be one. We all have 1,001 things we would like to do or get to make things better. Well, do them!

Make it a point to periodically review this book and other organizational texts for fresh ideas. IBT has an e-learning application (E-PEP) that you can easily access through your computer that may prompt some ideas and ways to take you to a new level of effectiveness. Continuous learning results in continuous improvement.

Include these objectives in your weekly plan. Schedule them. You will discover that you tend to figure out how to get them done in the least amount of time. Because the task is there, you act on it. Better yet, gradually and continuously your office is not only keeping its new image and efficiency, it is improving it.

You are making change part of your everyday life. And you are the one directing the change.

## PERIODIC CATCH-UP

Some people don't feel the need to maintain their organization minute-by-minute. They may not care to. They have successfully kept pace with their workload by periodically catching up on their organization. If in the middle of a project or peak period they will keep up as best they can, at the end of it they can spend the time they need to get themselves back in order. Here are a few important things to consider if you decide to work this way: Do not allow more than a couple of weeks to go by before you get reorganized. You should be very thorough about your cleanup. Keep very good reminder systems in place so important things don't fall between the cracks.

## MINIMUM MAINTENANCE

Once you're organized, the minimum maintenance you should do (which is better than nothing) is to clean off your desk each day before you go home.

## WHAT TO DO WHEN IT ALL GOES TO POT

So okay, you have purged your desk and office, and it looks like the cockpit of an F-16 aircraft. You are organized like never before. You finally got into a routine that keeps your day-to-day flow of paper, messages, information, e-mail, and so forth under control. You plan your work each Friday. You bought a notebook computer and have begun to learn an organizing software, and you feel pretty good about yourself. You are cruising along and bang—you run into a brick wall! You are called to Tokyo to replace a colleague for six weeks. Or a big customer puts your account up for review, and you need to prepare a presentation to salvage it, so for two weeks straight, 16 hours a day, you are dealing with that. Or you go on vacation and come back to backlogs and a mess all over again. Something like this will happen to you. And let me tell you, you'd better be clever with how you respond.

In my experience, people do not fall back into their *new* ways. No, chances are they slide back into old habits. And face it, you managed to cope using your old ways, right? It has probably been a real struggle to get organized. To have to do PEP all over again! It was a good try, but you're just not the organized type. Believe me, I have heard all of these. Don't despair or give up. There is an easy and painless way to deal with this. Have a *Do It Now* day. Put a sign on your door saying you are off for the day, clean up the papers on your desk—put them away where they belong—empty your e-mail inbox, update your task list, clean out the documents on your computer (in other words, go through the whole process again!). It is much easier and takes far less time than the first time you did it: Maybe a few hours and it is all under control again.

To make this *Do It Now* day easier, try to keep up with your daily flow of information anyway. If you are having to spend your days getting the presentation prepared, take an hour of that time and blast through what has come in the day before. Delegate liberally, then and there. Be decisive (even ruthless) about what you are not going to do. Take advantage of the circumstances to see how efficient you can be, and when you are back to normal keep that same pace!

It may never get this bad for you. But the workflow usually shifts at times and you may find yourself beginning to drown. One client, a director of one of the largest industrial firms in the world, described it this way:

*When work builds up and momentarily gets on top of me, I know what to do to deal with it because I have learned the necessary procedures.*

You now have learned the procedures, too.

Maintenance means recognizing the inherent cycle within every piece of work you do, from preparing yourself to do the work to putting everything back where it belongs after the work is completed, and guaranteeing that everything is in as good or better condition than when you first picked it up. Maintenance means organizing yourself while you work.

The most important thing to maintain is change for the better.

## FOLLOW-UP FOR CHAPTER 12

**1.** Recognize maintenance as the most basic and practical of work routines, and you'll be guaranteed a smoothly operating system for years to come. Make it a point to practice basic, practical maintenance routines that will guarantee the hard work you've put in to "get PEPed" will pay off for years to come.

**2.** Make your maintenance routines automatic, exactly in the same planned way you change the oil in your car. It's worth your time and effort to establish nonthinking, daily routines to maintain yourself and to maintain an organized state. Failure to maintain the system will result in an inability to work at all.

**3.** Have systems in place that will prevent you from falling back into old ways. Have routines that trigger continuous personal improvement and help you maintain those systems as a matter of course. Schedule this maintenance into your week.

**4.** Remember to think of work to be done in terms of work cycles. Each piece of work has a beginning, middle, and end. The task beginning includes preparing and setting up for the task. In the middle is the act of doing the task. Along with task completion, the ending includes maintenance points, including putting things back where they belong, and improving the condition of everything you touch, including files, tools, and so forth.

**5.** Realize that the advent of the computer means paper files aren't the only things that require maintenance. We now have computer files, and e-mail, as well. Maintaining your hard drive means having backup systems and using them regularly, so your electronically stored data isn't at the mercy of a sudden power failure.

**6.** Set a weekly organizing time to keep your long-term flow of work under control. Spend time each week planning for the coming week and maintaining your organized state. Get your filing up-to-date. Back up your hard drive. Check on your supplies. Use a quarterly, annual, or other schedule for maintenance to keep your maintenance on track and up-to-date.

**7.** If you discover you're spending time maintaining something you seldom use, seriously question its worth to you. If the reason you're maintaining something doesn't make sense to you, let that be a red flag to you. Ask why you're maintaining it. If it's something you can honestly do without, do without!

**8.** Organize yourself while you work. Make maintenance a part of the planning process, and you'll be including it from step one to step done. Plan for success. Establish good habits. Make maintenance a nonthinking habit, and you'll find it's an easy step on your road to success.

**9.** Don't get comfortable! Your real goal should be continuous improvement in everything you do. PEP is a tool, or a framework, to allow you to accomplish it.

# Just One New Habit

*What characterizes a well-adjusted person is not chiefly the particular habits he holds, but rather the deftness with which he modifies them or responds to changing circumstances. He is set to change, in contrast to the more rigid, dogmatic, self-defensive individual who is set to sit tight.*

—WENDEL JOHNSON

You may find very little profound thought in these pages, but there is a great deal of experience.

In essence, we have discussed the way you have conditioned yourself to approach your work: your habits. Most people will tell you (and I daresay too many of us believe) that it is very difficult to change habits. It isn't easy. But it can get better. It is possible to adopt new ways of doing things, to develop new habits in your life. You may have experienced walking into a new restaurant out of curiosity or by accident, and having found that you like it, you may make it a point to return again and again.

It all begins by adopting one new habit—taking action. *Do It Now* when the idea crosses your mind to test out a new method for doing your work.

The bad habit isn't necessarily being messy. The bad habit includes constantly neglecting the habit's correction—never doing a thing about it. Break that cycle and act on it now rather than postponing. You will find you'll have it licked in no time. It's up to you to act on your ideas as they occur. You will discover you can indeed be the master of your habits.

# RECOMMENDED READING

Allen, David. *Getting Things Done!* New York: Penguin Books, 2001.

Becker, Franklin, and Fritz Steele. *Workplace by Design*. San Francisco: Jossey-Bass Publishers, 1995.

Bettger, Frank. *How I Raised Myself from Failure to Success in Selling*. New York: Simon & Schuster, 1947.

Bittel, Lester R. *Right on Time*. New York: McGraw-Hill, 1991.

Bliss, Edwin C. *Getting Things Done: The ABC's of Time Management*. New York: Scribner, 1976.

Bruce, Andy, and Ken Langdon. *Do It Now*. New York: DK Publishing, 2001.

Covey, Stephen R. *The 7 Habits of Highly Effective People*. New York: Simon & Schuster, 1989.

Drucker, Peter F. *The Effective Executive*. New York: Harper & Row, 1966.

Dyszel, Bill. *Microsoft Outlook 2002 for Dummies*. Hoboken, NJ: John Wiley & Sons, 2001.

Ellis, Albert, and William J. Knaus. *Overcoming Procrastination*. New York: Signet, 1979.

Ellwood, Mark. *Cut the Glut of E-Mail*. Toronto: Pace Productivity, 2002.

Fiore, Neil. *The Now Habit*. New York: Penguin Group, 1989.

Fiore, Neil. *The Now Habit*. 2nd ed. New York: Penguin Group, 2007.

Gookin, Dan. *PC's for Dummies*. Foster City, CA: IDG Books, 1996.

Gray, Albert E. N. "The Common Denominator of Success," www.theintellectualviewpoint.com/reading/thecommondenominatorofsuccess-albertengray.pdf

Haberman, Scot, Andrew Falciani, and Scott Haberman. *Mastering Lotus Notes R5*. San Francisco: Sybex, 1999.

Hafner, Katie, and Matthew Lyon. *Where Wizards Stay Up Late: The Origins of the Internet*. New York: Simon & Schuster, 1996.

Hedrick, Lucy H. *365 Ways to Save Time*. New York: Hearst Books, 1992.

Hill, Napoleon. *Think and Grow Rich*. New York: Fawcett Crest, 1960.

Hobbs, Charles. *Time Power*. New York: Harper & Row, 1987.

Jenks, James M., and John Kelly. *Don't Do. Delegate!* New York: Ballantine Books, 1985.

Jensen, Bill. *Work 2.0: Rewriting the Contract*. New York: Perseus, 2002.

Knaus, William. *Do It Now: How to Stop Procrastinating*. New York: Prentice-Hall Press, 1979.

Kraynak, Joe. *The Complete Idiot's Guide to Computer Terms*. Indianapolis, IN: Alpha Books/Macmillan Computer Publishing, 1994.

LeBoeuf, Michael. *Working Smart: How to Accomplish More in Half the Time*. New York: Warner Books, 1979.

Lehmkuhl, Dorothy, and Dolores Cotter Lamping. *Organizing for the Creative Person*. New York: Crown Trade Paperbacks, 1993.

Londergan, Stephen, and Pat Freeland. *Lotus Notes 5 for Dummies*. Hoboken, NJ: John Wiley & Sons, 1999.

Mackenzie, R. Alec. *The Time Trap*. New York: McGraw-Hill, 1972.

Mayer, Jeffrey J. *Time Management for Dummies*. Foster City, CA: IDG Books, 1995.

McCay, James T. *The Management of Time*. Englewood Cliffs, NJ: Prentice-Hall, 1959.

McGee-Cooper, Ann, and Duane Trammell. *Time Management for Unmanageable People*. New York: Bantam Books, 1993.

Morgenstern, Julie. *Never Check E-Mail in the Morning*. New York. Simon & Schuster, 2004.

Morris, Larry. *E-Mail and Messaging*. Indianapolis, IN: New Riders Publishing, 1994.

Negroponte, Nicholas. *Being Digital*. New York: Vintage Books, 1995.

Nelson, Stephen L. *The World Wide Web for Busy People*. Berkeley, CA: Osborne/McGraw-Hill, 1996.

Peters, Thomas J., and Robert H. Waterman Jr. *In Search of Excellence*. New York: Harper & Row, 1982.

Peterson, Jim, and Roland Smith. *The 5S Pocket Guide*. Portland, OR. Productivity Press, 1998.

Petrick, Jane Allen. *Beyond Time Management*. Palm Beach, FL: Informed Decisions International, 1998.

Pocket Mentor. *Running Meetings*. Watertown, MA: Harvard Business School, 2006.

Schlenger, Sunny, and Roberta Roesch. *How to Be Organized in Spite of Yourself*. New York: New American Library, 1989.

Senge, Peter M. *The Fifth Discipline*. New York: Doubleday/Currency, 1990.

Seymour, Jim. *Jim Seymour's PC Productivity Bible*. New York: Brady/Simon & Schuster, 1991.

Winston, Stephanie. *Getting Organized*. New York: Warner Books, 1978.

# INDEX

# About the Institute for Business Technology

**The Bridge between Human Behavior and Technology**

Should you wish to download free copies of any of the forms found throughout this book, please see our company web site at www.ibt-pep.com or write or call:

> The Institute for Business Technology International, Inc.
> P.O. Box 1057
> Boca Raton, Florida 33429, USA
> Telephone (1) 561-367-0467
> Fax (1) 561-367-0469
> E-mail ibtint@ibt-pep.com

If you would like more information about the Personal Efficiency Program, E-PEP (our e-learning PEP application), or any of our other services, or if you would like to speak with a PEP representative, contact one of the following IBT offices.

If you have any questions for the author or are interested in having Kerry Gleeson speak at your company please see www.kerrygleeson .com

For those of you who have completed PEP, IBT has an offer for you—Our Global Promise.

What is the "PEP Global Promise"? It is IBT's promise that our colleagues who deliver PEP worldwide will provide ongoing, virtual support to any PEP graduates, wherever in the world they work. It's free, it's global, and it's our pleasure.

How can the "PEP Global Promise" help you? You may have participated in PEP at one stage of your career and then changed roles or even countries. If a regrounding in the PEP principles would help you succeed in your new situation, contact us.

How do our PEP graduates tap into the "PEP Global Promise"? When you need help, contact the IBT office closest to your location.

Are there any restrictions? Since the support is virtual, all you need is a phone number or an e-mail address. With that, IBT Worldwide can easily keep our "PEP Global Promise."

**IBT Argentina**
Besares 2268—(1429)
Buenos Aires
Argentina
Telephone/Fax (54) (11) 4704-9151
E-mail consultas@ibt.com.ar
Web site www.ibt.com.ar

**IBT Asia Pacific**
PEPworldwide
Level 10
56 Berry Street
North Sydney NSW 2060
Australia
Telephone (61) 2 9955 3333
Fax (61) 2 9955 5480
E-mail ibtap@pepworldwide.com
Web site www.pepworldwide.com

**IBT Australia**
PEPworldwide
Level 10
56 Berry Street
North Sydney NSW 2060
Australia
Telephone (61) 2 9955 3333
Fax (61) 2 9955 5480
E-mail australia@pepworldwide.com
Web site www.pepworldwide.com

**IBT Austria**
c/o IBT Europe
P.O. Box 17
2420 AA Nieuwkoop
The Netherlands
Telephone +31 172407592
Fax +31 172407592
E-mail info@ibteurope.com
Web site www.ibteurope.com

**IBT Belgium**
209 Rue des Romains
L-8041 Bertrange
Luxembourg
Telephone +352 308997
Fax +352 305228
E-mail info@ibtconsult.com
Web site www.belux.ibt-pep.com

**IBT Brasil**
Rua Dr. Carlos Augusto de Campos,
170/cj. 133
CEP 04750-060—São Paulo—SP
Telephone +55 11 55483389
Fax +55 11 55245181
E-mail ibtbrasil@gmail.com
Web site www.ibt-pep.com.br

**IBT Canada/Puerto Rico**
78 Donegani, Suite 210
Pointe-Claire, Quebec
Canada H9R 2V4
Telephone (514) 426-2325
1 (800) 631-9207 (Canada only)
Fax (514) 426-4986
E-mail info@ibtcda.ca
Web site www.ibtcda.ca

**IBT France**
P.O. Box 339
CH–1224 Chjne-Bougeries
Geneva
Telephone +41 22 869 11 00
E-mail ibt@ibt.fr
Web site www.ibt.fr

**IBT Germany**
c/o IBT Europe
P.O. Box 17
2420 AA Nieuwkoop
The Netherlands
Telephone +31 172407592
Fax +31 172407592
E-mail info@ibteurope.com
Web site www.ibteurope.com

**IBT Iceland**
Nethylur
110 Reykavik
Iceland
Telephone +354 578 1500
Fax +354 578 1510
E-mail info@ibt.is
Web site www.ibt-islandi.is

**IBT Japan**
IMPACT (Japan) Ltd.
2Fl, MF Bldg.
1-6-12, Yoyogi
Shibuya-ku
Tokyo 151-0053
Japan
Telephone (81) 3 5371 6677
Fax (81) 3 5371 6682
E-mail info@impact-japan.com
Web site www.impact-japan.com

**IBT Luxembourg**
209 Rue des Romains
L-8041 Bertrange
Luxembourg
Telephone +352 308997
Telephone +46 11 13 37 17
Telephone +32 2 3444 755
Mobile +352 021 15 99 54
E-mail info@ibtconsult.com
Web site www.ibt.lu

**IBT Netherlands**
Voorweg 97 AA
2431 AN Noorden
The Netherlands
Telephone +31 172407592
Fax +31 172407592
E-mail info@ibtbnl.nl
Web site www.ibt-pep.nl

**IBT New Zealand**
PEPworldwide
Level 4
19 Great South Road
Newmarket Auckland
New Zealand
Telephone (64) 9 529 1740
Fax (64) 9 529 1741
E-mail newzealand@pepworldwide.com
Web site www.pepworldwide.com

**IBT Norway**
Vardevn. 13A
N-1440 Drobak, Norway
Telephone (47) 64936210
Fax (47) 64936219
E-mail johan@ibtgruppen.no
Web site www.ibtgruppen.no

**IBT Poland**
IBT Polska Sp. z o.o.
ul. GórnoÊlàska 4A/80
00-444 Warszawa
Poland
Telephone +48 691 666 887
E-mail beata.uytenbogaardt@ibt-pep.pl
Web site www.ibt-pep.pl

**IBT Scandinavia A/S**
Lyngsoe Alle 3
2970 Hoersholm
Denmark
Telephone (45) 4925 1494
E-mail info@ibt-scandinavia.com
Web site www.ibt-scandivania.com

**IBT Singapore**
d'Oz International Pte Ltd
7500A Beach Road
The Plaza #10-301
Singapore 199591
Telephone (65) 6391 3733
Fax (65) 6744 3733
E-mail consultancy@d-oz.com
Web site www.d-oz.com

**IBT Southern Africa**
52 Kent Avenue
Sandringham, 2192
Johannesburg
South Africa
Telephone (27) (0)11 485 1316
Fax (27) 0866 186 972
E-mail info@ibt-pep.co.za
Web site www.ibt-pep.co.za

**IBT Spain**
c/o IBT Europe
P.O. Box 17
2420 AA Nieuwkoop
The Netherlands
Telephone +34 91 536 04 02
Fax +34 91 554 30 03
E-mail info@ibteurope.com
Web site www.ibteurope.com

**IBT Sweden**
Kraketorpsgatan 20
431 53 Molndal
Sweden
Telephone (46) 31-7061950
Fax (46) 31-877990
E-mail info@ibt.se
Web site www.ibt.se

**IBT Switzerland**
P.O. Box 339
CH–1224 Chjne-Bougeries
Geneva
Telephone +41 22 869 11 00
E-mail ibt@ibt-pep.ch
Web site www.ibt-pep.se

**IBT U.K.**
c/o IBT Europe
P.O. Box 17
2420 AA Nieuwkoop
The Netherlands
Telephone +31 172407592
Fax +31 172407592
E-mail info@ibteurope.com
Web site www.ibteurope.com

**IBT Ukraine**
Vienna House
36, Vorovskogo str
Kyiv
Ukraine
Telephone +380 44 593 18 86
Fax +380 50 444 43 21
E-mail office@ibt-pep.com.ua
Web site www.ibt-pep.com.ua

**IBT US PEP Productivity Solutions,**
**Inc.**
1651 Scooter Lane
Fallbrook, CA 92028
Telephone (1) 760-731-1400
Fax (1) 760-731-1414
E-mail info@PEPproductivitysolutions
.com
Web site www.PEPproductivitysolutions
.com

This book is due for return on or before the last date shown below.

1 5 OCT 2009    - 9 JUN 2011

1 4 DEC 2009   - 3 OCT 2011

- 1 FEB 2010    2 4 OCT 2012

- 9 MAR 2010

2 2 APR 2010

1 4 OCT 2010

- 3 NOV 2010

1 8 NOV 2010

- 9 DEC 2010
- 6 JAN 2011

- 5 APR 2011